Computational Mania

Jason Earls

Pleroma Publications

Computational Mania

ISBN

Image information for front cover: Main file found at **Wikimedia Commons** web site. File:Fractal Heart2 5600x4200.jpg; Author: Randomness; Licensing Permission (Reusing the file): **Public domain**; (cover made by Jason Earls using this image).

Second Edition
1st: January, 2015 – Revised April, 2017
Pleroma Publications

Also by Jason Earls

Guitar Patterns, Licks, and More

Computing with Fermat

Shrieks of Desertion: Poems

The Lowbrow Experimental Mathematician

How to Become a Guitar Player from Hell

That Man is a Sinner

The Splendor and Squalor of Numbers

The Underground Guitar Handbook

You Will Be Amazed by the Entertainment

Mathematical Bliss

Numbers for Wittgenstein

Primitive Knife Manual (with Scene Williams)

Heartless Bastard In Ecstasy

Red Zen

Concrete Calculator-Word Primes

Morzan the Slayer Must Die

Math Freak

I Sin Every Number

How to Make Your Own Head Explode

*Crazy F*ck*r In Paradise*

A Cringe-Meister in the Bathos-Sphere

Cocoon of Terror

Zombies of the Red Descent

0.13610152128364555667891105120136 15...

Death Knocks

Contents

"I have not proved that the universe is, in fact, a digital computer and that it's capable of performing universal computation, but it's plausible that it is."
-Seth Lloyd

"I believe that scientific knowledge has fractal properties; that no matter how much we learn, whatever is left, however small it may seem, is just as infinitely complex as the whole was to start with. That, I think, is the Secret of the Universe." – Isaac Asimov

"The study of the infinite is much more than a dry, academic game. The intellectual pursuit of the Absolute Infinite is a form of the soul's quest for God. Whether or not the goal is ever reached, an awareness of the process brings enlightenment."
– Rudy Rucker

"The task is not so much to see what no one has yet seen, but rather to think what no one has yet thought, about that which everyone sees." – Erwin Schrodinger

"The trouble with integers is that we have examined only the very small ones. Maybe all the exciting stuff happens at really big numbers, ones we can't even begin to think about in any very definite way. Our brains have evolved to get us out of the rain, find where the berries are, and keep us from getting killed. Our brains did not evolve to help us grasp really large numbers or to look at things in a hundred thousand dimensions."
– Ronald L. Graham

"It's like asking why Beethoven's Ninth Symphony is beautiful. If you don't see why, someone can't tell you. I know numbers are beautiful. If they aren't beautiful, nothing is." -Paul Erdos

"If you think of your life as a kind of computation, it's quite abundantly clear that there's not going to be a final answer and there won't be anything particularly wonderful about having the computation halt." -Rudy Rucker

Computa-
tional
Mania

by
Jason
Earls

Preface

I first became enamored with computation when I stumbled upon the family calculator at around 8 or 9 years old. I remember randomly punching the buttons at first, but then gradually entering legitimate arithmetic operations and being amazed when a huge answer would appear on the screen. Seeing those large numbers arrive almost instantly at the push of a few small buttons was a definite thrill.

I didn't like doing long division or large multiplication problems by hand in school. I wanted a machine to do it. I liked the idea of telling a machine what you want, then in a split second the absolutely correct answer is gleaming right there in front of you. I wished I had a machine that when I asked it about any problem in my life, it would easily present me with the precise answer in a split second. Of course in our modern times the internet is very close to that, but far from being 100% accurate.

In college I took a couple of programming courses thinking they would be close to the type of calculator computations I enjoyed. Although I did like some computer programming and got decent grades, for the most part it was too tedious for me. I didn't like the idea of writing extremely long programs to perform tasks that were not mathematically oriented. I was more attracted to short scientific programs, or scripts full of simple commands, that solved one particular problem. With long programs that handled a whole conglomeration of different scenarios, too many things could go wrong and it seemed extremely tiresome to deal with everything.

Numbers and computation are also appealing to me because they represent the idea of absolute truth. In my opinion, nothing gets closer to pure unadulterated truth than simple numerical facts that nobody (sane anyway) can ever argue with. For example, if I compute the number of divisors of the 240th Fibonacci number:

numdiv(fibonacci(240)) = 1376256

and my computer program is correct, no rational person can argue that the answer is wrong. And they can compute the same thing and if their program is correct it must agree with my answer.

Furthermore, I love numbers and computation because they are not human. At certain points in my life, it seemed that almost every contact I had with a human being resulted in a painful experience. But nowadays that isn't the case; only on rare occasions does it seem that way.

In grade school I got into trouble for using a calculator to do my homework. The teacher never gave me a precise reason why I could not use a calculator, but I suspect it was the usual belief that if I relied on it too much and refrained from practicing hand calculation using only pencil and paper, over time it would hinder my mathematical ability. But I don't think using a calculator back then (or all through my education) stifled my mathematical development (if I ever developed anything at all), actually I think it helped me by increasing my interest in a subject most people find to be extremely dry, dull, and tedious (see the first chapter of my book *The Splendor and Squalor of Numbers* for more on the story of using a calculator for my homework.)

On many occasions I have dreamed of making an extremely important discovery or solving a famous real-world problem using only my brain plus the help of a powerful computational device. (My favorite problems are those that require a little bit of analysis coupled with a lot of computation to finish the proof.) Making a truly great discovery has not happened yet, but a few things I have found through computation I am rather proud of.

Thank you for buying this book. I hope you find something of value in it.

-Jason Earls
January, 2015

The Harvard Calculating Savant

We went looking for Weston. My programmer friend, Jay, and I. We wanted to see how Weston was doing since it was winter and he was homeless. We hadn't seen him in a few months. We took off on our bikes, headed up town to the corner of Main and Santa Fe streets. We knew Weston liked sleeping in the alley around there since it was fairly safe compared to the rest of the city. Last time we checked, Weston had made a little cardboard house for himself sort of hidden back in the alley.

Weston's full name was Weston Seymour Flintmaster the III and he was a former Harvard student, but now a hardcore alcoholic. He had studied mathematics at Harvard in the 90s, but got interested in (supposedly) trivial little number theory problems and mental calculation feats and they had kicked him out of Harvard because of it, which ruined his mathematics career.

Jay and I thought Weston was a truly amazing individual, the smartest person we had ever encountered. We knew of no one else in the city who had Weston's numerical and mathematical skills, and it seemed we were the only people who could truly appreciate him. Everyone else thought he was nothing but a dirty stinking drunken bum. My friend Jay was currently a programmer at a market research company who loved number theory, and

I had an interest in recreational mathematics. I had met Weston one day when I saw a math text in an alley laying by a dumpster, it was titled *Number Theory for Computing* by Song Y. Yan, and as I was leaning down to pick it up, someone yelled at me from behind: “Hey that's my book! Leave it alone!” It was Weston. I talked to him for awhile that day, learned quite a bit about him, and we sort of became friends.

Jay and I rode our mountain bikes to the previously mentioned alley and found Weston sleeping beside a dumpster, clutching a bottle of cheap wine in his hand, along with many Stroh's beer cans laying around. We could see his little cardboard house not far away, but for some reason he was sleeping outside it next to the dumpster. He had probably gotten really plastered the night before.

“Hey Weston, wake up!” I yelled. “We came to learn some mathematics from you!”

“Go away, I'm drunk,” he mumbled without even opening his eyes. He looked emaciated and was wearing a brown fur coat with a bright green stocking cap. Huge combat boots were on his feet and a battered text book was laying next to him on the ground.

“You're always drunk, Weston,” Jay said. “Come on, show us some of your sweet number theory problems, man. We didn't ride all this way for nothing. We want to experience some of your genius, dude.”

Weston loved it when people called him a genius. It rejuvenated his self-esteem, which had dwindled significantly since becoming homeless. Weston's eyes grew wide when he heard the word and he gradually staggered to his feet.

“Feel like doing any mental calculation feats today Weston?” I suggested.

“Nah, too trivial,” he came closer to us, wiping some snot off his beard, then tipping his wine bottle toward his lips, but no liquid came out.

“Hey, I read about a new number yesterday that I want to tell you about,” Jay said, pulling a little scientific calculator out of his pocket. “I heard about GOOGLE, not the normal number googol, which is 10 to the one hundredth power, but the upside down calculator prime GOOGLE that's spelled like the popular search engine. So Weston, here's my question for you. What's the square of the upside down calculator prime GOOGLE after it has been concatenated five times.”

Weston's eyes went insanely wide after the question was posed. His tongue whipped out of his mouth, his neck jerked and his entire body went into minor spasms. When his brain started working on a calculation, his body would go into almost violent convulsions and he had no control over himself whatsoever.

I parked my bike and went over and stood next to Jay as he punched in the problem on his calculator. It had a large display window for doing scientific calculations. We were ready to check Weston's answer.

It took about 30 seconds before Weston finally regained consciousness and he responded by saying, "That would be about 143648109377075106040835006563684996719267753538787809822081, I believe."

He pronounced each digit quickly yet carefully. We watched his mouth move and looked at his front teeth that were all yellow, cracked, and broken from getting beaten up by people who hated homeless individuals. When Weston finished reciting the last digit, we checked his solution against Jay's calculator:

? 379009379009379009379009379009^2
%18 = 143648109377075106040835006563684996719267753538787809822081

"Wow, you are fucking brilliant, Weston!" I shouted.

Let me pause in the story and explain something to the reader. Weston had of course heard of the number googol, 10^{100}, but he had never heard of the upside down calculator prime 379009, but having a thorough knowledge of prime numbers, his mind immediately went into overdrive working out what it could be. In no time he found 379009, realizing that if you type that number into a calculator, then flip it upside down, the digits on the display window look like they spell out the word GOOGLE (Weston saw all this in his mind without actually having to test it on a calculator). Next Weston simply stuck five of those numbers end to end to form one large number, then he squared it to arrive at the correct answer. Weston performed all of this activity in his brain at the mere statement of the problem.

"That was pretty trivial," Weston said. "Now I'd like to tell you guys about a problem I was working on last night. First, I will mentally search for primes of the form $379*10^n+9$ because at about 3AM I found a proof that a similar form of number was prime an infinite amount of times. I think after hearing about this new number you mentioned, the Google upside down calculator prime, which I had never heard of before, I may be able to adapt my proof of last night's number to fit this new form, which seems slightly nicer to me. I'm glad you guys told me about it."

He paused and did some mental calculation, gyrating and spasming around for a bit, almost biting his tongue a couple of times. Finally he returned to consciousness and said: "The first few *n* values that make $379*10^n+9$ a prime number are: 3, 6, 8, 9, 37, 44, 67, 111, 157, 289, ..."

Jay pulled out his smart phone and did a Google search on Weston's sequence of numbers. "Looks like somebody already beat you to that problem, Weston. Some Earls asshole. Here, have a look at this OEIS entry."

A159264 Numbers n such that 379*10^n+9 is a ("Google") probable prime.

3, 6, 8, 9, 37, 44, 67, 111, 157, 289, 1256, 1602, 2410, 2482, 2868, 3824, 3891, 6595, 8984, 9318, 10274, 45858, 59152, 86691 (list; graph; refs; listen; history; text; internal format)

OFFSET	1,1
COMMENTS	The prime number 379009 rotated by 180 degree reads "GOOGLE". This sequence gives n such that "GO...OGLE" with n-1 O's is prime.
REFERENCES	J. Earls, Mathematical Bliss, Pleroma Publications, 2009, pages 15-17. ASIN: B002ACVZ6O [From Jason Earls (zevi_35711 (AT)yahoo.com), Nov 21 2009]
LINKS	Table of n, a(n) for n=1..24. Jason Earls, Google-Primes Henri & Renaud Lifchitz, PRP Records
MATHEMATICA	Select[Range[3, 300], PrimeQ[379*10^# + 9] &] (* Arkadiusz Wesolowski, Oct 05 2011 *)
PROG	(PARI) for(n=0, 9e9, ispseudoprime(379*10^n+9) & print1(n", "))

“Whoa, that's neat!” Weston said excitedly (which was unusual for him) as he examined the screen. “Ah, the joy of discovering a mathematical entity that another number addict also thought was nice. It's a great feeling.”

A light snow began to fall. It was about 25 degrees outside. The alley smelled of oil and cafe grease. I shivered from the cold, then looked over at Weston's cardboard shack.

“Hey Weston, do you have enough blankets in your cardboard house?” I asked. “How have you been doing? Are you staying warm enough at night?”

He looked down and brushed at his fur coat. “Sometimes at night I start a fire in the dumpster there to get warm. But I can't burn it for long without attracting the police. I'm staying warm enough though. The alcohol helps keep me warm. It's my best friend, other than the numbers of course.”

Jay hadn't been paying much attention to our little conversation, he was still tapping away on his smart phone, trying out more calculations.

“Hey Weston,” Jay said. “I've got another problem that may interest you. I like factorial numbers. Isn't it cool how they have a lot of zeros at the end?” I looked over at Jay's screen, which Weston of course didn't have to look at since he could see the numbers perfectly in his mind's eye:

```
? for(n=1,26,print(n!))
1
2
6
24
120
720
5040
40320
362880
3628800
39916800
479001600
6227020800
87178291200
1307674368000
20922789888000
355687428096000
6402373705728000
121645100408832000
2432902008176640000
51090942171709440000
1124000727777607680000
25852016738884976640000
620448401733239439360000
```

“Notice how the zeros are increasing as the numbers grow larger, but that they aren't uniformly increasing. So Weston, tell us the largest factorial number you can find that has the largest amount of zeros, but not just at the end of the number, count all the zeros throughout the entire number's decimal expansion."

Weston closed his eyes and started thinking. His body did a few jerks and quakes, but the convulsions this time were much less intense than for the other problems.

"The zeros continue to increase rather uniformly, so the record number sequence of them is not very interesting, I'm afraid."

Jay quickly wrote a little program to calculate the records for increasing number of zeros in n!:

```
? P(10000)
5:1,7:2,12:4,18:5,19:6,20:7,22:8,25:9,28:10,34:11,37:12,38:16,50:19,57:20,61:26,
73:35,85:36,94:37,105:45,114:47,115:51,122:52,124:53,127:54,133:61,153:62,154:68
,162:70,172:73,176:75,182:79,185:81,186:83,194:87,203:91,213:95,216:102,241:104,
249:105,254:114,257:120,264:121,273:133,285:135,304:142,327:155,337:159,345:160,
353:166,357:172,394:174,395:191,402:193,420:194,425:197,426:198,433:202,439:205,
442:215,450:216,469:227,481:235,490:244,525:245,537:262,551:270,553:281,592:286,
607:298,622:302,629:304,636:320,663:322,670:330,673:334,679:338,715:352,722:363,
724:364,735:368,738:370,755:374,775:384,798:388,800:397,812:403,819:406,838:419,
859:423,865:436,889:450,906:475,964:481,984:483,985:488,986:492,993:498,1002:500
```

The data above means that, for example, 19! has 6 zeros throughout its decimal expansion:

19! = 121645100408832000

Weston had been doing further mental calculations and finally he stopped and said. "Although this sequence is rather bland, I will tell you that the first factorial to have over 1000 zeros is 1868!, which has exactly 1008 zeros throughout its decimal expansion."

Jay let his program run a little longer and finally saw this:

1799:949,1815:964,1829:973,1868:1008,

“Wow!” Jay shouted. “It's incredible! He only used his brain for that. Fucking hell man! You're definitely a true genius all right. How do you do it?”

Weston grinned. He loved the attention he was receiving. It was hard being homeless. People usually either ignored him, beat him up, or insulted him so much he felt like shit most of the time.

“I have no explanation for it,” Weston said. “I just see the numbers in my mind. I always have.”

“So Weston,” Jay said. “Did you like studying math at Harvard?”

Weston slightly scoffed since he thought it was a stupid question, then he said: “Of course I did, it was an incredible experience. I learned a massive amount of number theory. My favorite thing was finding a problem that I could really get into, then just staying up in my dorm room working on it while periodically glancing out my window at the beautiful Harvard campus below. I could just wallow in the pure abstract bliss of mathematics while being at the most prestigious college in America. I loved being in my small room, totally isolated, working on number theory problems. I wasn't much of a social person. I also loved the feeling of being at Harvard in the winter time with snow falling and me warm inside at my desk working on a problem. Harvard had been a dream of mine ever since I was a child. Attending Harvard and studying mathematics there was the best time of my life."

"Did you graduate from there?" I asked.

"Sure did. I received my bachelors degree, but I didn't get to finish my masters. I was working on it when the trouble started."

"What trouble is that?" Jay said. "What happened to you?"

"Well, they say I began working on little computational number theory problems that were not worthwhile. They said I was spending too much time on them and neglecting my other studies; and it got so bad they had to boot me out of college. But I still don't agree that the math problems I worked on were trivial. I actually had another problem, a personal problem, that was much more serious, which prevented me from working on mathematics that they deemed important."

"And what problem was that?" I said.

"Well, on one occasion I agreed to see a psychiatrist, hoping by doing that they would let me stay at Harvard longer. Over the course of a few weeks the shrink got me to reveal a story about something that happened to me when I was about ten years old. I was living with my mother, she was single, had just gotten divorced from her third husband. And on this particular day my mother had decided to put some NAIR cream on her face to get rid of some light facial hair that had sprouted up. She of course didn't want any hair on her face and had applied this NAIR hair removal product to get rid of it, but the stuff was making my mother's face burn like hell. I guess the chemicals in it worked to simply melt the hair off a person's face, which can't be very safe. So after she washed it off, her face was still very sore. I was playing with some rubber bands at the time, flicking them around the room, setting up little targets and knocking them down with the rubber bands. And on a whim, when my mother walked by, I casually aimed the rubber band at her face and flicked it at her. Normally I would always miss, but just my luck, on this day I hit her. The rubber band fired directly into her burningly sore face from the NAIR, and she exploded on me. She ran toward me and started double-slapping me. *Right hand, left hand, right hand, left hand. Slap! Slap! Slap! Slap! Slap! Slap!* It hurt like hell and I was crying. But of course I deserved it. I shouldn't have been shooting rubber bands at my mother's face, especially if it was already burning badly from that dangerous NAIR product."

Jay shook his head back and forth. "That's an unfortunate story, Weston. I'm sorry that happened to you. But... I don't see how this relates to your math work."

"Well, all of a sudden out of nowhere in college, any time I would make a mistake while doing work on a so-called 'important' math problem, I would see and feel my mother double-slapping me and it would cause me to go a little bonkers. Pretty soon, every time I made the least little error in the math work I was supposed to be doing at Harvard, I would feel my mom double-slapping me and see her angry face cussing me and I would fully relive all the pain of that rubber band NAIR incident. However, on the little number theory problems I worked on in my spare time, I never got that feeling. I felt only peace and tranquility and lightness of being. The psychiatrist said the double-slapping incident is the source of all my problems. He said that's why I couldn't become a professional mathematician, and that I'll probably never be able to do serious mathematical work ever again. And I suppose I believe him, because that problem has never went away. But for some odd reason, it only appears on the really serious mathematics that they prefer at Harvard, never on any of the recreational or number theory problems that I like to do."

"Wow, what a story, Weston," I said. "That's really too bad. But I still think you're an awesome mathematician. You'll do really important work again, I know you will."

"Thanks." He lifted up his empty wine bottle again and tried to take a drink. Then he looked down at the ground and a thoroughly depressed look came over his face. "Ah well, what can you do?" he said with a shrug of his shoulders.

"Do you need anything, Weston?" I said. "Want us to bring you anything?"

In the past I had given him a sleeping bag and some cans of food, plus a bit of money here and there.

"How about a bottle of wine?" he said with a grin.

"I think you can get enough of that on your own," Jay said.

"Besides alcohol, is there anything you need?" I asked.

"Nah, I think I'm good to go guys," Weston said. "I just stocked up on some cans of beef stew and chili in my little house there. Just put a new roof on the place too, how do you like it?"

He pointed to his cardboard house and we looked at a blue tarp laying over the top of it.

"Looks great," Jay said.

Weston raised his gloved hand and stroked his beard a couple of times. "And I've also been working on a book."

"What!" I said. "You're working on a book?"

"Yes indeed. Just a little book of problems that interest me. I hope it turns out well."

"How are you writing it?" Jay asked. "Do you have a laptop in your cardboard house?"

"Nope, don't need one. Just a notebook and a pencil. I don't require a computer of any kind, because I've got this." His hand covered with a tattered glove pointed up to his brain. "When I'm finished, I'll pay someone to type it up for me, then hopefully get it published and make some money. I might even succeed in getting myself out of the poor house with this little book." He grinned showing his bad teeth.

"That's a great idea, Weston." I said. "I can't wait to read your book. Jesus, I bet it'll be amazing. Hey, have our questions about number theory problems inspired you at all to do this book?"

"Hmm, maybe."

I reached into my back pocket and pulled out a fifty dollar bill and offered it to him. He eagerly accepted it and stuck it in the pocket of his dirty fur coat. I knew he would buy alcohol with it, but in a few days I would bring him some other supplies that would be good for him.

"Thanks for the mathematics, Weston." I said. "You're the smartest man we've ever met. We'll be seeing you again soon."

Weston waved and walked over to his little cardboard house and I watched him slowly crawl inside. Then Jay and I got on our bikes and rode off.

Iterating Summation of Digits of Divisors to Reach 15

Try out this little iteration problem and see if you like it:

1. Pick a number bigger than 1.
2. Write down all of its divisors.
3. Find the sum of all the digits of the divisors.
4. Iterate this process until you arrive at a single number you can't break away from.
5. That number will always be 15.

Rather surprising, isn't it? Let's do an example. Using the number 35, it requires just three iterations to reach 15 since 35 -> 1+5+7+3+5 = 21 -> 1+3+7+2+1 = 14 -> 1+2+7+1+4 = 15. Sweet.

I won't provide a proof that **every number** will eventually reach 15 under this summation of digits of divisors process (I think I have only one proof in this entire book, other than visual numerical answers – if you consider those proofs – and that's the way I like it). Nevertheless, we can still perform some monster calculations to hopefully find something interesting about this iteration process. But first let's see the actual sequence entry for this problem as it appears in the OEIS:

A086793 Iterate the map n -> **sum of digits of** all divisors **of** n (cf. A034690); sequence gives number of steps to reach 15.

5, 4, 3, 9, 8, 2, 1, 11, 12, 5, 7, 10, 1, 0, 13, 12, 15, 6, 1, 2, 12, 9, 9, 11, 1, 13, 9, 8, 14, 10, 14, 8, 16, 3, 17, 6, 10, 2, 14, 9, 9, 2, 3, 9, 16, 8, 3, 3, 3, 16, 2, 12, 4, 16, 4, 2, 14, 1, 10, 2, 1, 15, 7, 3, 18, 2, 18, 10, 18, 12, 11, 6, 10, 17, 10, 10, 17, 13, 10, 11, 16, 8, 2, 14, 10, 15 (list; graph; refs; listen; history; text; internal format)

OFFSET 2,1

COMMENTS Ecker states that every number eventually reaches 15. "Take any natural number larger than 1 and write down its divisors, including 1 and the number itself. Now take the **sum of** the **digits of** these divisors. Iterate until a number repeats. The black-hole number this time is 15." [Ecker]

REFERENCES M. W. Ecker, Number play, calculators and card tricks ..., pp. 41-51 of The Mathemagician and the Pied Puzzler, Peters, Boston. [Suggested by a problem in this article.]

Good enough. Examining the terms of the sequence above, notice how even small numbers can require quite a few iterations to hit 15. Take 10 for example, here is its full trajectory:

```
? {m=10; stop=30; c=0;
while(c<stop, print1(m ", ");
c++; m=sumdigdiv(m);)}
10, 9, 13, 5, 6, 12, 19, 11, 3, 4, 7, 8, 15, 15, 15, 15, 15, 15, 15, 15, 15, 15,
 15, 15, 15, 15, 15, 15, 15, 15,
```

So 10 requires 12 full iterations before it hits 15. Can we find other numbers that require even more iterations before they arrive at the “black hole” number 15? Of course, but first let's see the sequence of new record iterations as it appears in the OEIS:

A095347 n sets a new record for number of iterations of the sum of digits of the divisors of n needed to reach 15 (see A086793).[3]

2, 5, 9, 10, 16, 18, 34, 36, 66, 162, 924, 71820, 127005777360 (list; graph; refs; listen; history; text; internal format)

OFFSET	1,1
COMMENTS	32320399999676796 takes 22 iterations to reach 15, but it probably is not the next term.
LINKS	Table of n, a(n) for n=1..13.
CROSSREFS	Cf. A034690, A086793. Sequence in context: A046711 A191171 A191776 * A249353 A224866 A159073 Adjacent sequences: A095344 A095345 A095346 * A095348 A095349 A095350
KEYWORD	more,nonn,base
AUTHOR	Jason Earls (zevi_35711(AT)yahoo.com), Jun 03 2004

Whoa. Look at the difference between the 12th and 13th terms, amazing! And the entry states that the gigantic number 32320399999676796 takes 22 iterations! Could we find a number requiring 23 iterations before it hits 15? I can tell you right now: that will be a very difficult thing to accomplish. But we can try. First, let's examine the data for how factorials behave under this iteration process:

```
? for(n=1,50,print1(n":"bh15(n!)", "))
1:-1, 2:5, 3:8, 4:9, 5:16, 6:18, 7:12, 8:4, 9:5, 10:6, 11:13, 12:19, 13:21, 14:2
0, 15:6, 16:18, 17:7, 18:12, 19:7, 20:4, 21:12, 22:4, 23:19, 24:14, 25:17, 26:16
, 27:12, 28:16, 29:12, 30:16,
```

My computer bogs down very much once it hits the "20s" when computing factorials. I doubt it would have made it to 50. When the divisors grow too plentiful, the computer stops the program and spits out an error message. Nevertheless, looking at the data above, we see that 13! requires 21 iterations to reach 15. That's very close to our

22 iteration record. But I'm still here to tell you, beating 22 will be extremely hard.

Here is the full trajectory for 13! under the black hole 15 iteration scheme:

```
? {m=13!; stop=30; c=0;
while(c<stop, print1(m ", ");
c++; m=sumdigdiv(m);)}
6227020800, 30990, 162, 66, 36, 46, 18, 30, 27, 22, 9, 13, 5, 6, 12, 19, 11, 3,
4, 7, 8, 15, 15, 15, 15, 15, 15, 15, 15, 15,
time = 43 ms.
?
```

Isn't it impressive how quickly the large starting number drops to a 3-digit number? That is the reason it's so difficult to find a number needing 23 steps to reach 15: the sum of digits of divisors function drops large numbers to their knees in no time flat!

What would happen if we simply took 13! and added successive numbers to it and then applied our iteration process to hopefully find a number requiring 23 iterations?

Examine this data and then I'll explain what is going on:

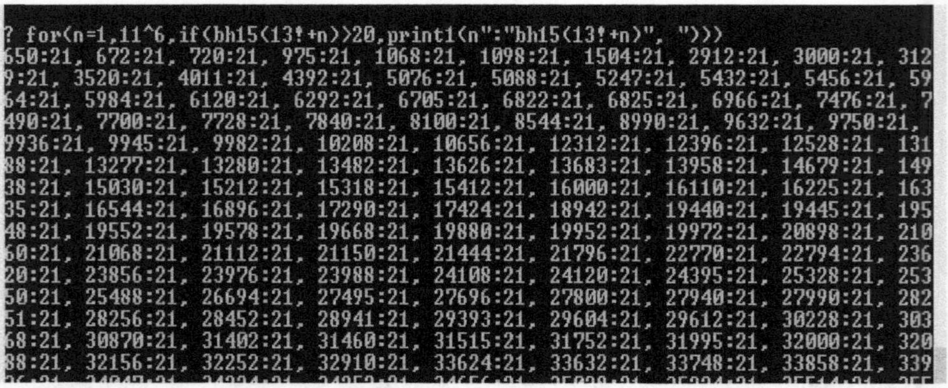

```
? for(n=1,11^6,if(bh15(13!+n)>20,print1(n":"bh15(13!+n)", ")))
650:21, 672:21, 720:21, 975:21, 1068:21, 1098:21, 1504:21, 2912:21, 3000:21, 312
9:21, 3520:21, 4011:21, 4392:21, 5076:21, 5088:21, 5247:21, 5432:21, 5456:21, 59
64:21, 5984:21, 6120:21, 6292:21, 6705:21, 6822:21, 6825:21, 6966:21, 7476:21, 7
490:21, 7700:21, 7728:21, 7840:21, 8100:21, 8544:21, 8990:21, 9632:21, 9750:21,
9936:21, 9945:21, 9982:21, 10208:21, 10656:21, 12312:21, 12396:21, 12528:21, 131
88:21, 13277:21, 13280:21, 13482:21, 13626:21, 13683:21, 13958:21, 14679:21, 149
38:21, 15030:21, 15212:21, 15318:21, 15412:21, 16000:21, 16110:21, 16225:21, 163
35:21, 16544:21, 16896:21, 17290:21, 17424:21, 18942:21, 19440:21, 19445:21, 195
48:21, 19552:21, 19578:21, 19668:21, 19880:21, 19952:21, 19972:21, 20898:21, 210
60:21, 21068:21, 21112:21, 21150:21, 21444:21, 21796:21, 22770:21, 22794:21, 236
20:21, 23856:21, 23976:21, 23988:21, 24108:21, 24120:21, 24395:21, 25328:21, 253
50:21, 25488:21, 26694:21, 27495:21, 27696:21, 27800:21, 27940:21, 27990:21, 282
51:21, 28256:21, 28452:21, 28941:21, 29393:21, 29604:21, 29612:21, 30228:21, 303
68:21, 30870:21, 31402:21, 31460:21, 31515:21, 31752:21, 31995:21, 32000:21, 320
88:21, 32156:21, 32252:21, 32910:21, 33624:21, 33632:21, 33748:21, 33858:21, 339
```

Look at all those 21 values! Above I am simply adding ever increasing values of *n* to 13! and computing how many steps they take to reach 15, then filtering out the ones that are less than 20 iterations. Notice an abundance of 21s appear but not a single 22. ***Running a search for values more than 21 did not turn up a single 22 value or greater!***

IT ALMOST SEEMS LIKE THERE IS SOMETHING SPECIAL ABOUT THE NUMBER 21 REGARDING THIS PROBLEM.

But there isn't. Because remember in the OEIS entry we saw a value listed that takes 22 iterations. They are just hard to find.

Moving on, let's try Fibonacci numbers and see how they behave:

```
? for(n=1,50,print1(n":"bh15(fibonacci(n))", "))
1:-1, 2:-1, 3:5, 4:4, 5:9, 6:1, 7:10, 8:2, 9:16, 10:16, 11:16, 12:14, 13:12, 14:
9, 15:18, 16:11, 17:10, 18:19, 19:15, 20:18, 21:18, 22:5, 23:9, 24:15, 25:9, 26:
18, 27:11, 28:4, 29:10, 30:16, 31:16, 32:17, 33:15, 34:11, 35:4, 36:12, 37:4, 38
:4, 39:15, 40:4, 41:17, 42:18, 43:10, 44:3, 45:12, 46:17, 47:11, 48:17, 49:2, 50
:11,
time = 126 ms.
```

These are much easier to compute than the factorials. And there are some fairly high values found as well.

```
? for(n=1,10^60,if(bh15(fibonacci(n))>18,print1(n":"bh15(fibonacci(n))",")))
18:19,60:19,74:20,105:20,108:21,128:19,130:20,148:19,150:20,151:19,155:20,164:21
,180:20,189:21,220:20,228:20,231:21,239:19,241:20,247:19,251:19,254:21,271:19,27
2:20,286:20,288:19,290:20,294:19,295:20,301:19,308:19,318:20,319:19,320:19,326:2
0,330:19,334:21,337:20,341:21,343:20,348:20,349:19,350:19,353:19,355:19,
```

The picture above shows data for those requiring at least 19 iterations to reach 15. Notice Fibonacci(108) requires 21.

Attempting the same experiment to see if we can reach at least a 22 iteration value (not even considering a 23), we will first examine the full trajectory of Fibonacci(108):

```
? {m=fibonacci(108); stop=30; c=0;
while(c<stop, print1(m ", ");
c++; m=sumdigdiv(m);)}
16641027750620563662096, 162882, 168, 102, 36, 46, 18, 30, 27, 22, 9, 13, 5, 6,
12, 19, 11, 3, 4, 7, 8, 15, 15, 15, 15, 15, 15, 15, 15, 15,
time = 112 ms.
```

Imitating my method earlier, I took the value of Fibonacci(108) and added ever increasing values of *n* to it to see how many steps were needed to reach 15, but I filtered out the ones less than 20.

```
(onacci(108)+n))>20,print1(n":"bh15(fibonacci(108)+n)",")))
90:21,264:21,329:21,336:21,381:21,508:21,558:21,591:21,626:21,661:21,749:21,884:
21,890:21,936:21,1002:21,1083:21,1408:21,1530:21,1638:21,1640:21,1764:21,1802:21
,1893:21,2000:21,2033:21,2036:21,2078:21,2188:21,2428:21,2714:21,2804:21,2862:21
,2970:21,2999:21,3158:21,3488:21,3524:21,3874:21,4054:21,4122:21,4284:21,4476:21
,4482:21,4494:21,4532:21,4707:21,4794:21,4802:21,4962:21,5018:21,5044:21,5136:21
,5304:21,5308:21,5464:21,5472:21,5664:21,5722:21,5760:21,5904:21,5981:21,6002:21
,6191:21,6196:21,6268:21,6272:21,6284:21,6480:21,6625:21,6634:21,6867:21,6884:21
,7020:21,7094:21,7182:21,7191:21,7200:21,7204:21,7316:21,7524:21,7758:21,7808:21
,7854:21,7944:21,8224:21,8424:21,8576:21,8598:21,8616:21,8713:21,
```

So we can see we're once again in the same boat as with the factorials. A barrage of 21s show up but not a single 22 value! What the frig is going on? Oh well, I give up.

I told you it would be difficult to find a 22 or greater. This iteration process is not easy to tame. It seems simple to find numerous values that require 21 iterations, but then locating a value that requires *just one more iteration* is where we have to bridge a large computational gap for some reason. I really don't understand why that would be the case.

I believe this problem really boils down to being a **computer memory and processing power** problem since if we could just put in a large enough number with the computer being able to handle the factorization and the total amount of divisors, then it may be easier to find one requiring more than 22 iterations. Nevertheless it does seem like there is something special about the amount of 21 iterations since they constantly show up yet 22 iterations do not appear.

Conjecture: Not until the year **2500** or beyond will someone be able to find a number requiring at least **100**

iterations to reach 15 under the sum-of-digits-of-divisors iteration process described in this chapter.

Can you think of any polynomials to try that might hopefully produce a 22 solution or greater? Conduct some experiments of your own to see what you can discover.

'60000006' Found in the Decimal Expansion of Pi^e

The decimal expansion of Pi^e begins like so:

22.459157718361045473427152204543735027 5...

This number is of course irrational, but only conjectured to be transcendental, meaning it is never the root of any algebraic equation (*more technical: "not a root of a non-zero polynomial equation with rational coefficients."* *-from Wikipedia*).

Last Saturday night, instead of hanging out with friends or family, I was having a wonderful time scanning through the decimal expansion of Pi^e. At one point I noticed something quite compelling and unusual among the digits: around the 45314th decimal place (I could be off by a few), there is a fascinating pattern lurking there, which is this:

60000006

Six zeros surrounded by two 6s. If you don't believe it's

really there, here's a picture of part of the decimal expansion of *Pi*^{e}; examine the last row carefully:

```
14229936342899273117047009151830457218013690633569583529646381273703277141155743
84941769423371395418079805492582829408671728851215456115412260529825712308014102
62170903011394726526243393762700833455399808289731956504727577901133085817939718
89410963528236878021545243169576998405679320603269280141397335688227754220740374
33190603182030759597492833156128956464215840595236439058426711648873210564977041
33987025624171527351463124689419776965169147606705881043717543545186051067059406
2315345627674070633850543240977737960000006504743374567193095
```

Do you see the pattern I'm talking about? Isn't it amazing that six zeros surrounded by two 6s can actually occur in the decimal expansion of *Pi*^{e}?

I wonder what it means? Is it like a double-rainbow? Does it have any deep mystical significance that we could possibly use to gain insight into the secret of life, or the mysteries of the universe? I doubt it. The pattern probably doesn't even have any significant *mathematical* meaning, let alone philosophical or mystical meaning. It's just a coincidence because anything could eventually occur among all those digits. Nevertheless, I still think it's utterly fantastic that it's there.

During that glorious Saturday night when I had so much fun scanning through the decimal expansion of *Pi*^{e}, I also noticed a few other symmetrical patterns among the digits (I won't give the exact locations for these; you can compute the number and discover them for yourself if you are so inclined):

800008

500006

977778

377773

300004

Perhaps as more digits of Pi^e are computed, the amount of consecutive zeros increases? No. I don't really believe that's true. But I will do this:

Conjecture: At some point in the decimal expansion of Pi^e, two n's, one on each side, of n zeros will always be found. For example, at some point these strings will all eventually occur: 700000007, 8000000008, 90000000009, 1000000000000010, 1100000000000011, 120000000000000012, 13000000000000000013, ... etc.

Concerning the sequence mentioned in the conjecture, around the 775th decimal place, the pattern '101' occurs. But that is easy to find. The second term '2002' will be more difficult.

Did you know that digit-hunting is greatly looked down upon by serious mathematicians? Some think it's really a disgusting activity and even quite ludicrous. But I don't mind though. I still love digit-hunting simply because it's such a fun activity for a hardcore geekazoid like myself.

So this is just a short chapter about one little numerical curiosity I found, with an added conjecture. Not every chapter of this book has to be cram-packed with hardcore mathematical results, does it? Can you find any other interesting patterns in the decimal expansion of Pi^e?

Primes Made from Powers of Ten and Fibonacci Numbers

Fibonacci numbers have intrigued people for centuries.

```
? for(n=0,66,print1(fibonacci(n)", "))
0, 1, 1, 2, 3, 5, 8, 13, 21, 34, 55, 89, 144, 233, 377, 610, 987, 1597, 2584, 41
81, 6765, 10946, 17711, 28657, 46368, 75025, 121393, 196418, 317811, 514229, 832
040, 1346269, 2178309, 3524578, 5702887, 9227465, 14930352, 24157817, 39088169,
63245986, 102334155, 165580141, 267914296, 433494437, 701408733, 1134903170, 183
6311903, 2971215073, 4807526976, 7778742049, 12586269025, 20365011074, 329512800
99, 53316291173, 86267571272, 139583862445, 225851433717, 365435296162, 59128672
9879, 956722026041, 1548008755920, 2504730781961, 4052739537881, 6557470319842,
10610209857723, 17167680177565, 27777890035288,
```

An interesting problem is raising powers of ten to progressively larger values and then searching for the least Fibonacci number such that when it's added to the power of ten it becomes a prime number.

```
? for(n=0,20^3,k=1;while(!isprime(10^n+fibonacci(k)),k++);print1(n":"k", "))
0:1, 1:1, 2:1, 3:7, 4:16, 5:4, 6:4, 7:16, 8:47, 9:8, 10:31, 11:4, 12:56, 13:16,
14:31, 15:23, 16:64, 17:4, 18:4, 19:16, 20:17, 21:104, 22:82, 23:136, 24:1624, 2
5:7, 26:32, 27:904, 28:31, 29:47, 30:47, 31:64, 32:16, 33:16, 34:82, 35:44, 36:4
7, 37:47, 38:73, 39:4, 40:32, 41:217, 42:47, 43:23, 44:56, 45:184, 46:92, 47:64,
 48:152, 49:128, 50:119, 51:104, 52:122, 53:124, 54:271, 55:8, 56:4, 57:136, 58:
26, 59:74, 60:52, 61:233, 62:74, 63:64, 64:104, 65:73, 66:143, 67:97, 68:194, 69
:64, 70:23, 71:34, 72:31, 73:148, 74:217, 75:364, 76:49, 77:8, 78:47, 79:394, 80
:266, 81:7, 82:346, 83:104, 84:146, 85:356, 86:106, 87:247, 88:239, 89:1274, 90:
353, 91:386, 92:16, 93:106, 94:26, 95:124, 96:136, 97:103, 98:322, 99:424, 100:4
4, 101:4, 102:1364, 103:386, 104:23, 105:4, 106:263, 107:4, 108:559, 109:248, 11
0:191, 111:64, 112:1039, 113:136, 114:271, 115:143, 116:122, 117:553, 118:343, 1
19:298, 120:593, 121:304, 122:41, 123:4, 124:34, 125:16, 126:164, 127:128, 128:2
57, 129:487, 130:344, 131:128, 132:152, 133:8, 134:122, 135:3146, 136:41, 137:44
, 138:2431, 139:866, 140:7, 141:448, 142:7, 143:263, 144:112, 145:98, 146:97, 14
7:16, 148:322, 149:28, 150:1772, 151:386, 152:7, 153:316, 154:146, 155:116, 156:
719, 157:464, 158:113, 159:887, 160:392, 161:167, 162:364, 163:1546, 164:296, 16
5:3184, 166:226, 167:154, 168:1679, 169:17, 170:824, 171:188, 172:266, 173:418,
174:736, 175:287, 176:191, 177:196, 178:122,
```

For example, look at the numbers for the fourth term

given above: "3:7". This means that 10^3 + Fibonacci(7) is a prime number.

```
? 10^3+fibonacci(7)
%3 = 1013
? isprime(1013)
%4 = 1
```

It's surprising to me that when n=24 we have to go all the way up to the 1624th Fibonacci number before we can get a prime.

```
? 10^24+fibonacci(1624)
%5 = 1112865717198634453179949886009748282225121661022381839379509812788775864844
4481615142939909007389327472221774725997551943643434047894331958231815032597629
1375201108297782409166923187655116416820903980099852671450647413746275726315534956
8287149775027398833993078063424529308324664373994724063317223284996939768205969
31937274271321621474244 3
? isprime(%5)
%6 = 1
```

For those interested, here is more information on Pari's "isprime(x)" function.

```
? ?isprime
isprime(x,{flag=0}): true(1) if x is a (proven) prime number, false(0) if not.
If flag is 0 or omitted, use a combination of algorithms. If flag is 1, the
primality is certified by the Pocklington-Lehmer Test. If flag is 2, the
primality is certified using the APRCL test.
```

Another interesting anomaly in the sequence is when

n=165 and the 3184th Fibonacci number has to be added to make it a prime.

```
? 10^165+fibonacci(3184)
%9 = 116724374081495541233435764579214184068974717443439437236331282736262082452
385312960682327210312278880768244979876073455971975198631224699392309001139062 56
91096510740196510760817053932060237984793918970003774751244713440254679507687069
90550322971334370940093654442411815206857904041043400568568081194379503001967669
35663379234721865689613658399032791816735272116358165035957768655229310270882722
42471094763821154275682688200402585049861134087733332208736164591167264971986989
15791355883431385556958003121928147052087175206748936366171253380422058802655291
40335814561951460427946535764467290281171154076012677256157286715574607026067859
2297917904248853892358861771163
```

A fairly large prime indeed. Will every successive power of ten have a Fibonacci number associated with it such that it becomes prime when added? I believe every one will. Try to prove me wrong.

I like the terms of the sequence such that $k < 30$ for Fibonacci(k) because that means we can see a lot of zeros in the decimal expansion of the prime found.

```
? for(n=0,20^3,k=1;while(k<31 && !isprime(10^n+fibonacci(k)),k++);if(k<30,prin)
0:1, 1:1, 2:1, 3:7, 4:16, 5:4, 6:4, 7:16, 9:8, 11:4, 13:16, 15:23, 17:4, 18:4, 1
9:16, 20:17, 25:7, 32:16, 33:16, 39:4, 43:23, 55:8, 56:4, 58:26, 70:23, 77:8, 81
:7, 92:16, 94:26, 101:4, 104:23, 105:4, 107:4, 123:4, 125:16, 133:8, 140:7, 142:
7, 147:16, 149:28, 152:7, 169:17, 195:8, 265:26, 280:7, 291:7, 311:26, 334:17, 3
57:8, 367:26,
```

Notice the abundance of 4s and 16s above.

```
? 10^33+fibonacci(16)
%14 = 1000000000000000000000000000000987
?
```

Powers of ten and Fibonacci number primes are pretty sweet. Try to find some more.

1729 and Brilliant Numbers as Sums of Two Cubes

Hardy's story of Ramanujan and the number 1729. Man, I've heard it way too many times. Yeah, admittedly it's a great story. But what the hell. Anyone who is a mathematician (or just a bozo playing around with numbers like me), is familiar with this story. Yet people keep repeating it all the time.

I guess since it's so easy to understand from a mathematical standpoint, writers like to put it in their books. And of course it illustrates the genius of Srinivasa Ramanujan. He truly was a one-of-a-kind supreme mathematical genius. Some of the formulas and identities he managed to derive are completely out-of-this-world and thoroughly mind-blowing. Here is the Hardy story if by some miracle you have not heard it before:

From Wikipedia: "1729 is known as the Hardy-Ramanujan number after a famous anecdote of the British mathematician G. H. Hardy regarding a hospital visit to the Indian mathematician Srinivasa Ramanujan. In Hardy's words: 'I remember once going to see him when he was ill at Putney. I had ridden in taxi cab number 1729 and remarked that the number seemed to me rather a dull one, and that I hoped it was not an unfavorable omen. "No," he replied, "it is a very interesting number; it is the smallest number expressible as the sum of two cubes in two different ways.”'”

So after encountering this story yet again in a number theory text recently, I decided to try to program the basic problem of finding many numbers that are the sum of two cubes in at least two different ways. I thought it would be very easy to do and that solutions would be popping up on my computer screen in no time.

Wrong. It turns out to be a fairly hard problem for me to write code efficient enough to conduct a productive search in a reasonable span of time. I was surprised. After a few attempts at writing a decent little script and failing due to a lack of efficiency, I finally managed to rewrite the program well enough to locate the next taxi cab number after 1729, which is 4104.

It seems my programming skills leave a lot to be desired, which makes it difficult for me to find anything of mathematical substance. But I'm gonna keep trying.

So after finding the next term (4104) and then waiting for a long time for more, I had no luck and decided to just call it a day and go to the *Online Encyclopedia of Integer Sequences* to find out if the sequence of solutions already existed.

Here is a screen-shot of what I found:

1729,4104, Search Hints

(Greetings from The On-Line Encyclopedia of Integer Sequences!)

Search: **seq:1729,4104**

Displaying 1-3 of 3 results found. pag

Sort: relevance | references | number | modified | created Format: long | short | data

A001235 Taxi-cab numbers: sums of 2 cubes in more than 1 way.

1729, 4104, 13832, 20683, 32832, 39312, 40033, 46683, 64232, 65728, 110656, 110808, 134379, 149389, 165464, 171288, 195841, 216027, 216125, 262656, 314496, 320264, 327763, 373464, 402597, 439101, 443889, 513000, 513856, 515375, 525824, 558441, 593047, 684019, 704977 (list; graph; refs; listen; history; text; internal format)

OFFSET 1,1

COMMENTS From Wikipedia: "1729 is known as the Hardy-Ramanujan number after a famous anecdote of the British mathematician G. H. Hardy regarding a hospital visit to the Indian mathematician Srinivasa Ramanujan. In Hardy's words: 'I remember once going to see him when he was ill at Putney. I had ridden in taxi cab number 1729 and remarked that the number seemed to me rather a dull one, and that I hoped it was not an unfavorable omen. "No," he replied, "it is a very interesting number; it is the smallest number expressible as the sum of two cubes in two different ways."'"

Nice. It seems there are tons of solutions. (While I was browsing around on the web for more info on the original 1729 solution, I stumbled upon a page that said Bernard Frenicle de Bessy who lived from 1602-1675 had already found some of the solutions (seen above) way before Ramanujan, wow!)

Okay, so there has already been a lot of work done in this area. I don't need to do anything more. I need to change the problem and have my own fun. Why not. I still want to look for sums of two cubes, but need to have a certain class of number in mind that they can sum up to. I decided to go with brilliant numbers. I just really like that class of numbers for some unknown reason.

Brilliants are numbers that have exactly two prime factors of the same decimal length. For example, 19893641 is brilliant since it has just two factors of 4 digits each: 2237 * 8893. Here is their entry in the OEIS:

A078972 **Brilliant** numbers: semiprimes (products of two primes, A001358) whose prime factors have the same number of decimal digits.

4, 6, 9, 10, 14, 15, 21, 25, 35, 49, 121, 143, 169, 187, 209, 221, 247, 253, 289, 299, 319, 323, 341, 361, 377, 391, 403, 407, 437, 451, 473, 481, 493, 517, 527, 529, 533, 551, 559, 583, 589, 611, 629, 649, 667, 671, 689, 697, 703, 713, 731, 737, 767, 779, 781 (list; graph; refs; listen; history; text; internal format)

OFFSET 1,1

COMMENTS "**Brilliant** numbers, as defined by Peter Wallrodt, are numbers with two prime factors of the same length (in decimal notation). These numbers are generally used for cryptographic purposes and for testing the performance of prime factoring programs." [Alpern]

Brilliants are one of my favorite types of numbers. I have many classes of numbers that I love, but brilliants are definitely near the top of the list. At some point I would like to make an actual list of my all-time favorite types of numbers and put it into this book. In fact, I think I'll do it right now.

primes
brilliant numbers
repunits
semiprimes
fibonacci numbers
squares
triangular numbers
transcendental numbers
harshad numbers
cubes
irrational numbers
palindromes
perfect powers

That's really about it. I like other classes of numbers such as hailstone numbers, abundant numbers, smith numbers, and perfect numbers too, but they are much less malleable than those given above. Hence I can't work with them very often and they are not among my absolute favorites. I like numbers I can do something creative with. Those are the kind that are the most fun for me. I've gotten a lot out of my favorite classes of numbers too. I have learned a ton about number theory and mathematics simply by exploring their properties.

All right, enough rambling, back to our original problem. I performed a search for brilliant numbers that are also the sum of two cubes and here is the raw data I managed to pluck from the Platonic Realm:

```
break> FXB(9300,9300,9300)
1:2:9
2:1:9
2:3:35
2:9:737
3:2:35
3:10:1027
4:7:407
4:9:793
5:6:341
6:5:341
6:7:559
7:4:407
7:6:559
7:10:1343
8:9:1241
8:11:1843
9:2:737
9:4:793
9:8:1241
10:3:1027
10:7:1343
11:8:1843
```

The above means that $2^3 + 9^3 = 737$ and $11*67=737$ is a brilliant number. Simple enough. After running my program, it soon stalled out very quickly. Which is disappointing since the brilliants are not very large. I don't know what's happening. Perhaps the brilliants are getting so large they are difficult to factor? That can't be it since the program stopped at brilliants that have only two prime factors. Usually one has to arrive at a brilliant with quite a few digits before it completely halts the program. For example, here is data representing the sequence of least k values such that 10^n+k is a brilliant number (not counting squares):

```
? for(n=1,20,k=1;while(!isbril(10^n+k) ||
1:4,
2:43,
3:3,
4:403,
5:13,
6:22117,
7:43,
8:160063,
9:81,
10:2200057,
11:147,
```

So this program makes it up to 10^{12} before stalling out. What the data means is that, let's take the case for n=11, 147 is the first number after 10^{11} that makes it a brilliant number when added:

factor(10^11+147)

=

[281683]

*

[355009]

so we made it up to 6-digit factors before the program stalled. I suspect the reason we're not finding any more cubes that sum to a brilliant number is that there aren't any more solutions. I am going to try to think of a way to prove this. Wish me luck.

Nevertheless, returning to our list of solutions, here are all the solutions to "sum of two cubes equals a brilliant number (in one way only)" after the repetitions have been removed:

2*2*2 + 1*1*1 = 9 = 3*3
2*2*2 + 3*3*3 = 35 = 7*5
2*2*2 + 9*9*9 = 737 = 11*67
3*3*3 + 10*10*10 = 1027 = 13*79
4*4*4 + 7*7*7 = 407 = 11*37
4*4*4 + 9*9*9 = 793 = 13*61
5*5*5 + 6*6*6 = 341 = 11*31
6*6*6 + 7*7*7 = 559 = 13*43
7*7*7 + 10*10*10 = 1343 = 17*79
8*8*8 + 9*9*9 = 1241 = 17*73
8*8*8 + 11*11*11 = 1843 = 19*79

Conjecture: Two cubes summing to brilliant numbers in only one way are **finite**, and all the solutions ever to be found are given in the list above.

Now I'll end this chapter with some Gertrude Stein-like rumination:

Why aren't there any more solutions with larger prime factors? Surely solutions just slightly bigger wouldn't be too difficult to factor. There must be something else going on in the mysterious realm of the integers regarding this problem. I'll try to explore some other options and see what I can discover.

But time is running out. I want to get this book published. There's never enough time for all the projects I want to complete. But I really need to find out what's going on with this problem. Judging from the basic idea alone, my intuition would say there should be infinitely many. But the solutions definitely halt in a hurry. Why can't I find more? Why is the search stopping so suddenly? Are they really that hard to factorize? Surely there are more of them out there. Are they really finite? Judging from the behavior of the search it sure seems that way. Maybe my program is just so inefficient it's having a lot of trouble finding more.

Who knows. On to the next chapter.

On Factorials and Squares

One of my all-time favorite number theory problems is the Diophantine equation of adding one to a factorial to make it a square. It is so simple and pure. It's sublime. As far as I know, it remains unsolved to this day. If you are not acquainted with the exact formulation of this problem, it's known as Henri Brocard's factorial square problem and can be defined like so:

"Brocard asked if the only solutions to the equation $n! + 1 = m^2$, in positive integers (n, m), are (4, 5), (5, 11), (7, 71), this problem remains open." *-from Mactutor biography of Brocard*

After stumbling once again upon this problem in a book, a variant of it immediately popped into my mind: Are there any squares of the form $n! + k^2$? In other words, are there any solutions to the equation:

$$n! + k^2 = m^2$$

The fun part of asking questions such as this is getting to break out the old ghetto computer to do a few (non)mindless brute-force searches to hopefully find some solutions.

For me computation is always the best way to go.
Let's begin.

```
? R(300)
4        1      25
4        5      49
5        1      121
5        7      169
5        13     289
5        29     961
6        3      729
6        8      784
6        11     841
6        24     1296
6        31     1681
6        41     2401
6        57     3969
6        88     8464
6        179    32761
7        1      5041
7        12     5184
7        17     5329
7        39     6561
7        43     6889
7        52     7744
7        69     9801
7        76     10816
7        93     13689
```

Okay, so solutions do exist. Here are a few examples to better illustrate the data above:

$$4!+5^2 = 49 = 7^2$$
$$5!+13^2 = 289 = 17^2$$
$$6!+179^2 = 32761 = 181^2$$

Notice in the third example that the factorial number is smaller than the square value. $6! = 720$ and $179^2 = 32041$. I don't mind. Any and all solutions are welcome.

So are there infinitely many of these equations? I don't know. Running more brute-force tests revealed that the higher the value I used in the two "for loops" in my computer program, the more solutions were revealed.

For example, when both of the "for loops" have maximum search values of 2000, the search seems to end with this data:

11	585	40259025
11	685	40386025
11	764	40500496
11	828	40602384
11	996	40908816
11	1140	41216400
11	1258	41499364
11	1440	41990400
11	1557	42341049
11	1586	42432196
11	1758	43007364
11	1824	43243776
12	288	479084544
12	508	479259664
12	780	479610000
12	1125	480267225
12	1182	480398724
12	1800	482241600
13	288	6227103744
13	1160	6228366400
13	1710	6229944900
14	420	87178467600
15	464	1307674583296
16	1856	20922793332736

Then when I increase the "for loops" to end with 20000, the program seems to end with this data:

13	19744	6616846336
14	420	87178467600
14	4088	87195002944
14	4230	87196184100
14	4998	87203271204
14	7056	87228078336
14	8739	87254661321
14	10320	87284793600
14	13320	87355713600
14	13991	87374039281
14	14832	87398279424
14	15380	87414835600
14	16149	87439081401
14	17804	87495273616
14	18648	87526039104
14	19966	87576932356
15	464	1307674583296
15	3060	1307683731600
15	8433	1307745483489
15	9576	1307766067776
15	14670	1307889576900
16	1856	20922793332736
16	12240	20922939705600
17	10080	355687529702400

Notice by increasing the "for loop" ending values, we went from having only one solution in the 14 category, to having fifteen solutions in the 14 category!

What would happen if we raise the ending values to 100000? These values will be found:

15	76920	1313591054400
15	82026	1314402632676
15	85288	1314948410944
15	88560	1315517241600
15	91164	1315985242896
15	94428	1316591015184
15	96555	1316997236025
15	99540	1317582579600
16	1856	20922793332736
16	12240	20922939705600
16	33732	20923927735824
16	38304	20924257084416
16	58680	20926233230400
16	69065	20927559862225
16	70182	20927715401124
16	82080	20929527014400
16	84280	20929893006400
16	90560	20930991001600
17	10080	355687529702400
17	43728	355689340233984
17	59130	355690924452900
17	63735	355691490246225
17	94088	355696280647744
18	46848	6402375900463104

So for the 17 value, we went from one solution to having five.

Pretty slick.

How far can we push the computation?

Not far with my little trashy computer. But I'll see what I can do.

First, with ending values of 1000000 here is how the solutions begin:

```
? R(1000000)
4          1          25
4          5          49
5          1          121
5          7          169
5          13         289
5          29         961
6          3          729
6          8          784
6          11         841
6          24         1296
6          31         1681
6          41         2401
6          57         3969
6          88         8464
6          179        32761
7          1          5041
7          12         5184
7          17         5329
7          39         6561
7          43         6889
7          52         7744
7          69         9801
7          76         10816
7          93         13689
```

And here is how they seem to end:

```
17         930624   356553489125376
17         945440   356581284889600
17         984348   356656369081104
18         46848    6402375900463104
18         142962   6402394143861444
18         181440   6402406626201600
18         356621   6402500884265641
18         409080   6402541052174400
18         494613   6402618347747769
18         537858   6402662996956164
18         702720   6402867521126400
18         765504   6402959702102016
18         812560   6403033959481600
18         851040   6403097974809600
18         947160   6403270817793600
19         210240   121645144609689600
19         268520   121645172511822400
19         412020   121645270169312400
19         495072   121645345505117184
19         497181   121645347597778761
19         583064   121645440372460096
20         400320   2432902168432742400
20         897777   2432902814180181729
21         652848   51090942597919951104
```

Cool! Some pretty freakin' large squares in the far right column, eh?

Let's try just one more. With an ending value of 3000000 this time.

```
18        2663658 6409468779668964
18        2729040 6409821365049600
18        2877444 6410653389701136
18        2957472 6411120346358784
19        210240  121645144609689600
19        268520  121645172511822400
19        412020  121645270169312400
19        495072  121645345505117184
19        497181  121645347597778761
19        583064  121645440372460096
19        1002016 121646104444896256
19        1285056 121646751777755136
19        1428498 121647141015368004
19        1490160 121647320985657600
19        1777104 121648258507458816
19        2076840 121649413673217600
19        2255872 121650189367312384
19        2650155 121652123730356025
19        2842560 121653180556185600
20        400320  2432902168432742400
20        897777  2432902814180181729
20        1740760 2432905038422017600
21        652848  51090942597919951104
21        2286816 51090947401236857856
```

So with an increase of 2 million over our last value, we only managed to find one more 20 solution, and one more 21 solution! Sweet. But that's enough computation for now.

All right, since I can't seem to prove anything specific about this problem, I will offer up some philosophical speculation about what appears to be going on.

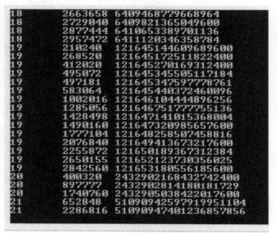

What our computation amounts to is simply taking two different classes of numbers and adding them together to find square numbers, and because we are not putting any restrictions on the size of the factorials being less or greater than the squares we are adding, it isn't really surprising that when we increase the ending values of the "for loops" that we are continuing to find more and more solutions.

Because what we are doing is simply taking two classes of numbers and combining them to find squares. Thus it seems possible that if we take any two big sets of numbers with no restrictions on size of either one, we can just keeping trying different cases until eventually we find some that when added together they are bound to be squares.

So the conclusion is that this is not a particularly interesting problem. But it was fun to explore. And it beats getting hammered on whiskey shots or shooting speed balls (cocaine and heroin mixture) into our veins, right?

The Famous Frank Cole Factorization and Repunits Squared Factorizations

I love the story of Frank Nelson Cole and his famous factorization. Legend goes that in 1903 Cole was giving a talk at the *American Mathematical Society* titled "On the Factorization of Large Numbers." When his turn came to speak he simply went to the blackboard and wrote out the following large number along with its two huge prime factors, all without saying a word to the audience:

$$2^{67}-1 = 147573952589676412927$$
$$193707721 * 761838257287$$

Although it took my computer only 236 milliseconds to find the prime factorization above, Frank Nelson Cole used the full hour of his talk to write out the calculations (multiplying the two factors together to show they perfectly agreed with the decimal expansion of $2^{67}-1$) in front of the audience members while remaining totally silent. When Frank Cole had finally written down all the correct digits, he simply went back to his seat, having never spoken a single word.

The audience went wild. The normally grim and staid mathematicians in attendance all cheered, clapped, guffawed, shouted "Bravo!", and some even wept openly with happiness and glee (only kidding) at what Frank Nelson Cole had taken many years to accomplish using only pencil and paper (not kidding).

After re-reading the famous Frank Nelson Cole story recently, I felt totally inspired and wanted to do some factorizations similar to what he had accomplished that fine day over 100 years ago. Except there was no way in hell I was going to use only a pencil and paper. Screw that bullsh*t. I was going to compute like a rabid dog slobbering at the mouth the whole time, since that's the only fun part about doing mathematics for me. If calculators and computers did not exist, I wouldn't be caught dead engaging in any kind of mathematical activity (kidding again, sorry).

So what kind of prime factorizations could I do that were similar to Cole's legendary one? Could I choose a simple little polynomial like 3^n+2 and find something interesting? Nope. I'm sure that form of number has been explored and computed to death by hundreds if not thousands of enthusiastic computational number theorists around the world. So I had to pick a more unusual form of number if I wanted to break new ground.

First, an explanation. Doing number theory, for me, is almost like a creative art. I'll start by getting an idea for something I want to try to find, and if the numbers do not cooperate at first, I can sort of shape and mold them to better fit my idea (or sometimes I'll adapt my idea instead of the numbers). But it almost seems like numbers are malleable since you can just bend and twist them to fit the problem you are working on.

Yes, most mathematicians judge this to be “contriving” a problem and say that it isn't “natural” to do mathematics in this way. And I have to admit I agree with them. Yet I don't care. Because it's too much fun for me to stop. (Notice that if people aren't trying to take your money in this world, they're trying to take away all your fun.) Contriving mathematical objects to me is almost like doing crack, once you get a little taste you can never get enough and you can't simply just stop doing it or you'll have serious withdrawal symptoms that are a thousand times more powerful than heroin (joking again). How do you like it now, gentleman? as Hemingway used to say.

All right. So a lot of people have already found the prime factors of traditional polynomials such as 3^n+2 or whatever, so I decided to use one of my favorite classes of numbers:

The Mighty Repunits

Repunits are simply repeating ones, like so: 1, 11, 111, 1111, 11111, 111111, 1111111, ... and they are given by the simple formula $r(n)=(10^n-1)/9$. I love repunits since they remind me of a person doing primitive counting arithmetic using basic marks, like this:

1 = |

2 = | + |

3 = | + | + |

4 = | + | + | + |
5 = | + | + | + | + |
etc.

Of course I realize this is not what repunits actually represent. But I still like to think of them this way. It seems so minimalist and pure and majestic.

So I decided to use repunits after they have been squared to hopefully find some interesting prime factors, but in the end I had to add 2 to the original numbers (shaping and molding) to stumble upon something cool.

Here is one nice prime factorization I found:

$$R(24)^2+2$$
$$=$$
$$12345679012345679012345654320987654320987654323$$
$$=$$
$$421098402246231374947$$
$$*$$
$$29317800652985419420183409$$

Wow, look at those huge prime factors! The famous Frank Cole factorization has 9-digit and 12-digit factors, while the ones above are 21-digit and 26-digit prime factors, respectively. Notice the decimal expansion of the main number. Squaring repunit numbers produces some nice "surface level" digital patterns, as you can see here:

```
? for(n=1,24,print(r(n)^2))
1
121
12321
1234321
123454321
12345654321
1234567654321
123456787654321
12345678987654321
1234567900987654321
123456790120987654321
12345679012320987654321
1234567901234320987654321
123456790123454320987654321
12345679012345654320987654321
1234567901234567654320987654321
123456790123456787654320987654321
12345679012345678987654320987654321
1234567901234567900987654320987654321
123456790123456790120987654320987654321
12345679012345679012320987654320987654321
1234567901234567901234320987654320987654321
123456790123456790123454320987654320987654321
12345679012345679012345654320987654320987654321
```

Next I decided to search for semiprimes (numbers with exactly two prime factors) among a slight alteration of the same class of numbers: $R(n)^2-2$, I subtracted 2 instead of adding 2. Here is what I found:

2, 3, 5, 6, 7, 10, 11, 12, 15, 19,
21, 23, 25, 27, 28, 31, ...

What the hell? Why are there so many?

Below is computer output listing the prime factorizations for the first 24 $R(n)^2-2$ numbers. Notice the far right column lists exactly how many prime factors each one contains.

```
? for(n=1,70,print(n":"factor(r(n)^2-2)":"bigomega(r(n)^2-2) ))
1:Mat([-1, 1]):0
2:[7, 1; 17, 1]:2
3:[97, 1; 127, 1]:2
4:[17, 2; 4271, 1]:3
5:[257, 1; 480367, 1]:2
6:[1249, 1; 9884431, 1]:2
7:[135449, 1; 9114631, 1]:2
8:[7, 1; 23, 1; 439, 1; 14449, 1; 120889, 1]:5
9:[8849, 1; 17599, 1; 79274369, 1]:3
10:[8782759, 1; 140567206841, 1]:2
11:[2747161, 1; 44939772412679, 1]:2
12:[47, 1; 2626740215387444418177, 1]:2
13:[71, 1; 38431, 1; 4524545366780709 19, 1]:3
14:[7, 1; 569, 1; 30995930234359608583393, 1]:3
15:[653045863, 1; 18904765670869358713, 1]:2
16:[18119, 1; 9367171417, 1; 7273983110689153, 1]:3
17:[1433, 1; 37887247, 1; 22739229318800737l7769, 1]:3
18:[17, 2; 5297, 1; 98207, 1; 18146144927, 1; 4525435149887, 1]:6
19:[8818754888393, 1; 13999344769854890l548983, 1]:2
20:[7, 1; 17, 1; 433, 1; 607, 1; 9884383, 1; 39933912977844151743093 7, 1]:6
21:[4801, 1; 257148073575206811337658563930868 3119, 1]:2
22:[2161, 1; 63889103, 1; 48121206431, 1; 18582190869505929950 3, 1]:4
23:[174884561, 1; 70593304187358648613615653006473 4079, 1]:2
24:[223, 1; 397721, 1; 2317271239, 1; 600695977830665877455498 16287, 1]:4
```

Observe that quite a few of them have very large prime factors. You know, there is just something phenomenal about cracking open numbers to find humongous prime factors. It always gives me a thrill for some reason.

Furthermore, $R(29)^2-2$ is actually a prime number:

123456790123456790123456790120
98765432098765432098765431 9

Here are more factorizations:

```
25:[23439930388763797919, 1; 52669435478629762559561295601, 1]:2
26:[7, 2; 839, 1; 126241, 1; 351920103811592737, 1; 67594667659419853368937, 1]:
6
27:[263, 1; 46941745294090034267474064591841524667887152044313, 1]:2
28:[28111, 1; 43917608809169645378484148589080940592211387748129, 1]:2
29:Mat([123456790123456790123456790120987654320987654320987654319, 1]):1
30:[23, 1; 91378546921, 1; 632529580297519, 1; 9286713707233913891693923663247,
1]:4
31:[15499985017417, 1; 79649619005909391977388624644742773119898897207, 1]:2
32:[7, 1; 103, 1; 3797402201, 1; 45091337611706373013949766656635958186538946476
439, 1]:4
33:[9187007, 1; 17071279, 1; 276285159169, 1; 2849163135618011370616453484502625
49567, 1]:4
34:[17, 1; 5113, 1; 111246409, 1; 1276745294825442713014670364289004327322558511
92404671, 1]:4
35:[2617, 1; 3167, 1; 6079, 1; 14208833, 1; 216888826183, 1; 7951251005068247090
71485637992825744641, 1]:6
36:[17, 1; 3610759, 1; 201125694761384599427395589490866520074072107467030697255
460873, 1]:3
37:[4447, 1; 7759, 1; 5053667113011789359739361, 1; 7080036040119575607928842435
559769728223, 1]:4
```

R(38)²-2, R(42)²-2, and R(43)²-2, seem fairly difficult to factorize. My computer stalled for quite a while on those numbers without splitting them open.

Here are six more factorizations:

```
? for(n=39,70,print(n":"factor(r(n)^2-2)":"bigomega(r(n)^2-2) ))
39:[737041, 1; 53348297, 1; 3139805699118676942205889149715431023974141178763878
14041439047, 1]:3
40:[226510871, 1; 11791394663, 1; 1808304605160580441, 1; 2556166666230516864283
33528593043458491783, 1]:4
41:[5399, 1; 684857, 1; 33388872563922184614762103690179316498462725490962423958
967478308920433, 1]:3
```

```
? for(n=44,70,print(n":"factor(r(n)^2-2)":"bigomega(r(n)^2-2) ))
44:[7, 1; 113, 1; 2603063, 1; 191679356119, 1; 1030286375753, 1; 7769494690073,
1; 39077587621763561757251138673082709063513, 1]:7
45:[127, 1; 1297, 1; 7817, 1; 3426831464836487, 1; 27979401876921714777894311344
65533984288241850684678629588984319, 1]:5
46:[647, 1; 3184943, 1; 59911340394274354316077640189717229723550435612878373286
8250162777804286239315639, 1]:3
```

Conjecture: There are infinitely many semiprimes of the form $R(n)^2-2$, but none of them will ever be brilliant numbers.

Just think, the work given in this chapter (admittedly quite trivial) was directly inspired by Frank Nelson Cole and his amazing factorization of $2^{67}-1$ using just pencil and paper that he presented way back in the year 1903 which took him "three years of Sundays" to perform. Most of the factorizations presented above took only a few minutes to find on a not-very-powerful home computer. Isn't technology wonderful?

Ten's Complements of Brilliant Numbers

Let's do another problem concerning brilliant numbers. Would there be anything wrong with that? Probably not. I told you I really like the brilliants.

First off, we need to know this: What is the ten's complement of a number? Say you have the number 23. The highest power of ten directly above 23 is of course 100. When you subtract 23 from 100 you get 77. And 77+23=100. So 77 is the ten's complement of 23. Simple enough. Do the same procedure with larger numbers and higher powers of ten.

Next, surely you know what a brilliant number is if you've made it this far in this book.

So the main question of this chapter becomes: Could there be any brilliant numbers such that their ten's complements are also brilliants?

Indeed there are; and it seems amazing to me that they actually exist. Once you see the data below, you will soon realize why I must conjecture that there are infinitely many of this form of numbers.

Here are the first brilliant numbers whose ten's complements are also brilliant:

```
? for(n=1,5*10^5,if(isbril(n) && isbril(tc(n)),print1(n",")))
4,6,221,473,527,779,979,12827,14933,17063,18203,22331,22577,24047,24797,25199,28
757,29591,29651,29747,30353,31979,33233,37391,37979,39059,39449,40217,41471,4169
3,42167,42401,42521,43709,43739,43847,44969,45047,45173,45431,46763,47573,47603,
48077,48899,49601,50399,51101,51923,52397,52427,53237,54569,54827,54953,55031,56
153,56261,56291,57479,57599,57833,58307,58529,59783,60551,60941,62021,62609,6676
7,68021,69647,70253,70349,70409,71243,74801,75203,75953,77423,77669,81797,82937,
85067,87173,94037,94937,96023,97133,97709,98171,98237,99101,99221,99677,99779,10
8419,112661,120983,148433,165911,168881,171737,185093,212519,236849,238067,24868
7,250247,285359,285653,287471,287663,317183,333083,345623,346517,355151,356393,3
69437,372599,373097,377879,388139,388511,388847,391649,402047,427319,433793,4339
19,441671,444359,453689,463637,473699,474689,
time = 3,425 ms.
?
```

I ran the program to a much higher level than shown above; and solutions kept popping up without them ever seeming to stop. I wish I could prove that there are infinitely many of these, but I wouldn't know where to begin. Let me think for a minute...

Nope, I see no way to reason that if you have one brilliant number, and on some occasions its ten's complement is also brilliant, that these will somehow continue indefinitely. I don't know how to prove something like that.

Let's stop the babbling and give an example of what the data above really means. Taking the first 5-digit term 12827 as an example, it's prime factors make it brilliant:

factor(12827) =

[101]

*

[127]

Then its ten's complement is 10^5-12827 = 87173,

and that number's prime factors also make it brilliant:

factor(87173)
[179]
*****
[487]

Rock on. Now what would happen if we made up a really strange brilliant sequence and tried to see if it actually existed. Let's say for a sequence we want to find brilliant numbers whose ten's complement are also brilliant and when we concatenate them together (stick them together end to end), they are prime numbers. That's definitely a bizarre sequence. Surely nothing like that could ever really exist...

Could numbers really be that weird? Of course they can. Look at this:

A084629 Brilliant numbers such that when they are concatenated with their 10's complement, which also must be brilliant, the result is a prime.

473, 779, 22331, 30353, 47573, 53237, 57599, 66767, 68021, 75953, 81797, 96023, 97133, 99221, 112661, 120983, 212519, 236849, 248687, 373097, 388511, 391649, 427319, 433793, 444359, 453689, 473699, 474689, 555641, 566081, 566207, 597953 (list; graph; refs; listen; history; text; internal format)

OFFSET 1,1

REFERENCES J. Earls, **Mathematical Bliss**, Pleroma Publications, 2009, pages 10-11. [From Jason Earls (zevi_35711(AT)yahoo.com), Nov 21 2009]

LINKS Table of n, a(n) for n=1..32.

EXAMPLE a(3)=22331 because it is a brilliant number and its 10's complement: 77669 is also brilliant and 2233177669 is prime.

Conjecture: The sequence above is infinite.

I came up with that sequence quite a few years ago and I had completely forgotten about it. Then when I started researching material for this chapter, I stumbled upon it once again and it was kind of shocking. The sequence seems peculiar yet also interesting due to the weird symmetry the terms contain. But I bet there are some real mathematicians out there who have seen it listed in the OEIS and shook their heads with pure disgust. Oh well. What can you do. You can't please everyone. I had no idea what I was thinking back then because I was a completely different person at that time of my life.

Moving on, it occurs to me at this point to engage in some philosophical speculation. Why do I do computational number theory anyway? Why will I go several months or years with no interest in mathematics, then all of a sudden I find myself immersed in a number theory phase so intense that I'm computing and conjecturing and examining walls of data and thinking about numerical properties nearly every minute of the day? I have no clue.

And what is it exactly I'm looking for? It seems to me I am searching for numbers that are like rare jewels hiding in the Platonic Realm that no one else has ever laid eyes on before; and once I find them I want to know if they are truly one-of-a-kind (finite), or if there are perhaps very many of them (infinite). By rare jewels I mean simply numbers with "interesting" properties (one or two pure basic facts), and once I find one, or a few of them, I want to know if they end, or continue on forever. Seems simple enough.

My interest in computational number theory really boils down to just that one simple notion. It's kind of sad that all of my "mathematical work" dwindles down to only that, but I'm afraid it's the only contribution I can make. (Good thing I can play guitar and record my own music as another creative outlet.)

But to reiterate, I'm just trying to find numerical objects with properties that I think are interesting, and then I try to gather evidence as to whether they are finite in nature, or infinite. Yep, it's kind of disappointing when I whittle it down to something so concise. But hopefully before I die I'll have discovered at least a few interesting mathematical ideas that someone may find intriguing or entertaining or learn something from. That's the most I can ever hope for, I suppose. It's good enough for me.

Fractal Art

FreeDictionary.com defines a fractal as, “an object whose parts, at infinitely many levels of magnification, appear geometrically similar to the whole. Fractals are used in the design of compact antennas and for computer modeling of natural-looking structures like clouds and trees.”

In the 80s and 90s, fractals were extremely popular and computer hobbyists generated thousands of them using fractal software. Since that time however, interest in fractals has waned considerably, due to most of the fractal equations having been fully explored (and nearly exhausted).

In this chapter I will provide some intriguing fractal images found at the *Wikimedia Commons* web site that were all listed as being in the public domain.

I have provided names for each of the fractals above the image and also given credit to the original creator.

"Fractal Eye of Morgoth" by Randomness:

"Hidden Mandarin Fractal" by Soler97:

"Fractal Art Bubbles" by Ralph Langendam:

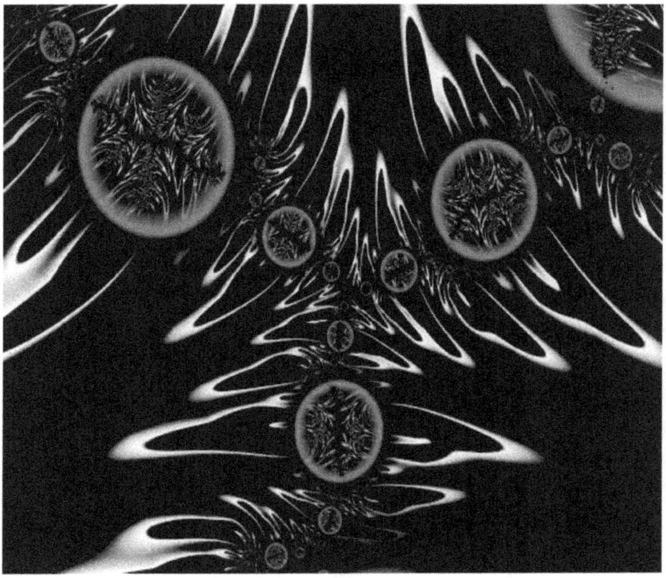

"Fractal Tower" by Soler97:

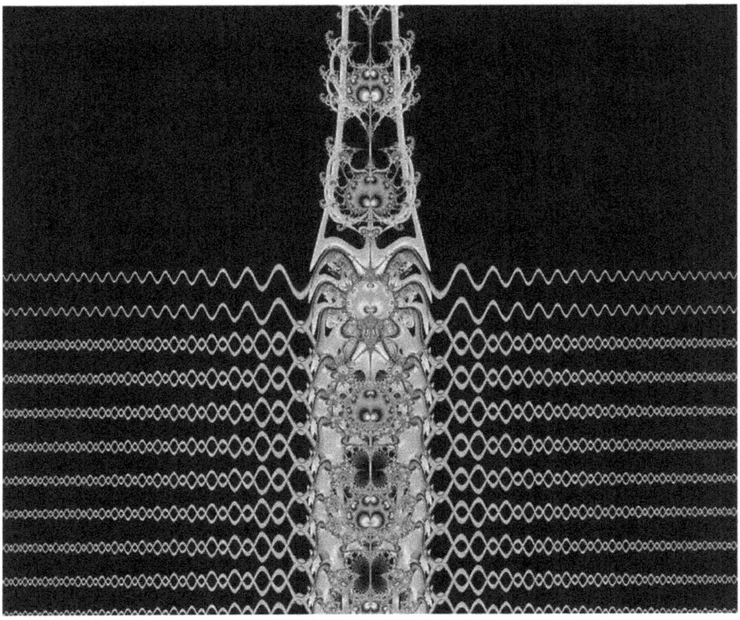

"Fractal Heart" by Randomness:

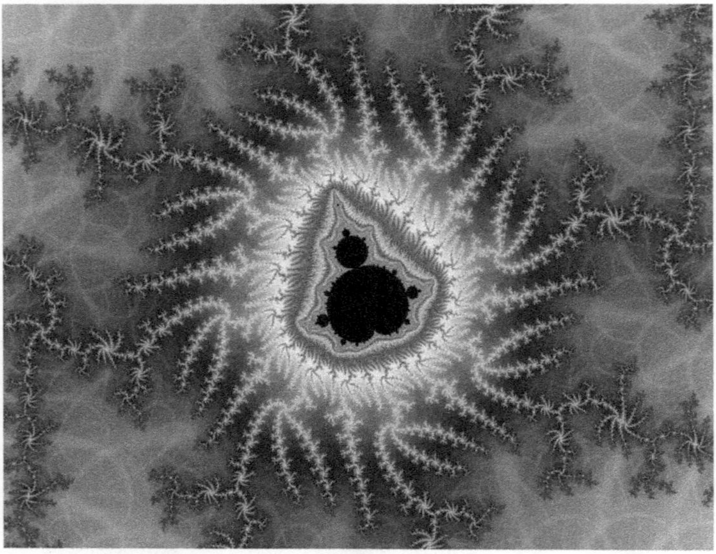

"Fractal Art" by Ralph Langedam:

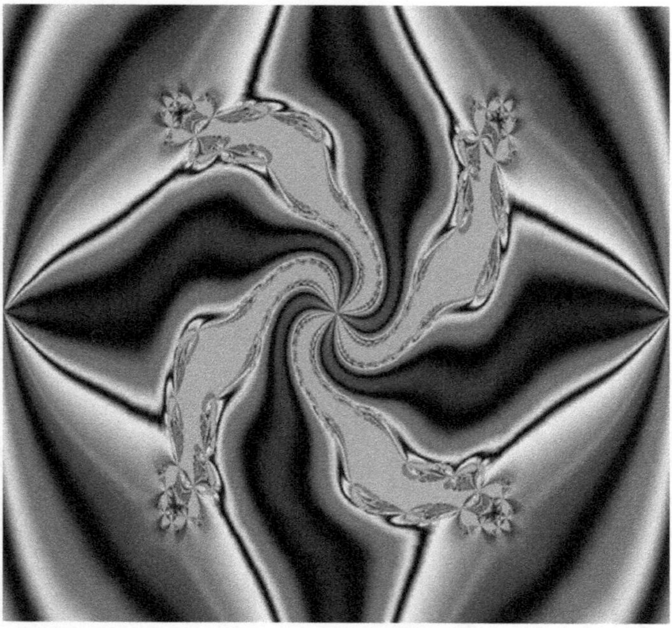

"Julia Fractal" by Bakasama:

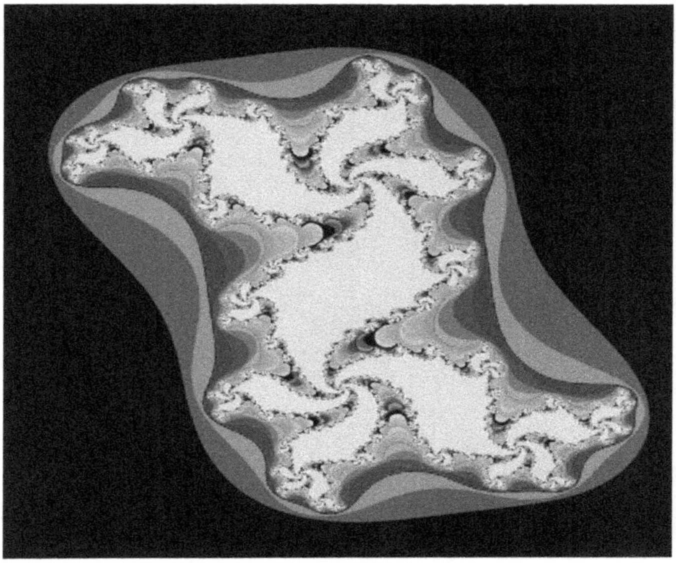

"Burning Ship Fractal" by Inductiveload:

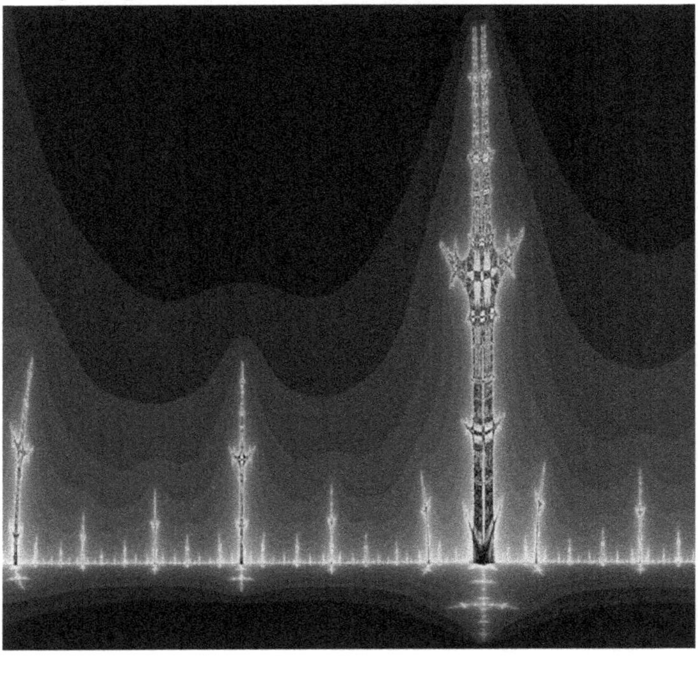

"Newton Fractal" by Georg Johann-Lay:

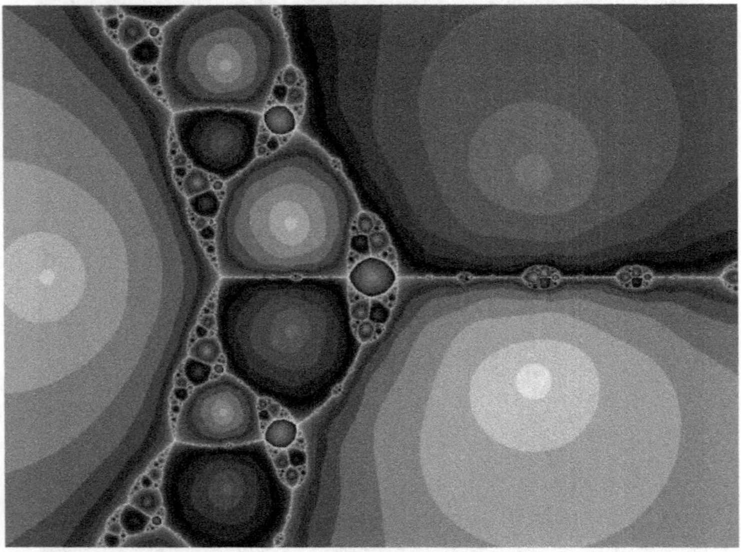

"Fractal Tentacle" by Randomness:

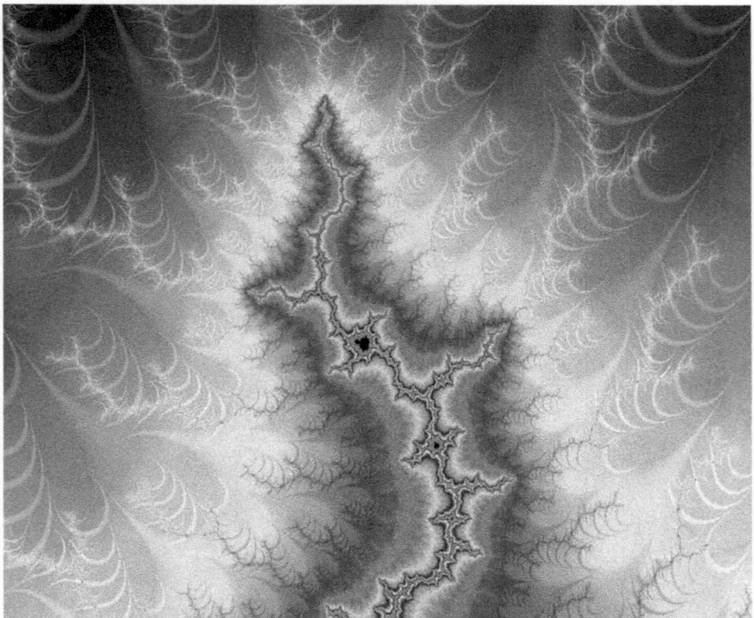

The 379009 Upside Down Calculator-Word Prime

[This chapter was adapted from my book Concrete Calculator-Word Primes *]*

Upside down calculator-words are tremendous fun for me. (These are simply numbers typed on a calculator display such that when the calculator is flipped upside down the sequence of digits resembles a normal alphabetic word.) I like calculator-words a little too much for my own good, because instead of doing serious mathematics (whatever that is), I spend a lot of time playing around with them.

A few years ago I discovered the stimulating fact that the calculator-word 379009 is a prime number (379009 spells "GOOGLE" when turned upside down on a calculator; and a prime number is a positive integer with no divisors other than itself and one). Ever since discovering 379009 I have enjoyed trying to find other calculator-word primes, since that was one of the coolest recreational math things I ever discovered (I even took it a step further and made a polynomial of $379*10^n+9$ to find more Google primes by enhancing the amount of zeros in the middle; you can find this sequence in the *Online Encyclopedia of Integer Sequences* as A159264).

Below is another way of adapting calculator-words to find prime numbers: you can put a border of digits around them. The main reason one would do this is that unfortunately not all calculator-words are prime numbers. After putting a border of digits around the calculator-word you like, then you can use the entire thing as a constant in a polynomial and add more digits to the end of it and then test to hopefully discover when the polynomial becomes prime through a simple process of elongation.

Remember that 379009 is actually a prime in itself, but below you will see a border has been added surrounding 379009 so that I could see what other kinds of primes would turn up through adding more digits to the end.

Here you go:

GOOGLE

```
1111111111111111
1000000000000001
1000037900900001
1000000000000001
1111111111111111
    00000001
```

The Google prime above has more prime values associated with it than the one given above (which is for *n*=8). If we let Z={111111111111111110000000000000 0110000379009000011000000000000001111111111111 1111} and conduct a search for primality on the polynomial Z*10^n+1 we find that it's prime when *n*=8, 22, 38, 40, 79, 289, 298, 398, 913, 1576; and probably more if you would like to continue the search. Also see sequence A159264 in the *OEIS*.

What other kinds of calculator-words can you put a border of digits around to find more primes?

(Palindrome*2+1) To Get Another Palindrome

Palindromes are numbers that read the same way forward and backward. For example, 1234321.

Palindromes are just simple little recreational number objects that don't have much mathematical significance, but they can be a nice break from studying brain-melting proofs that can be quite depressing when one can't understand anything in them; and occasionally it can be fun to just pay attention to the surface level of numbers.

While trying to listen to one of my relatives talking to me the other day, my mind wondered off and I thought: “Would it be possible to find a palindrome such that if we multiply it by 2 and add 1 this new number will also be a palindrome?”

I went home, ran to my computer, and found these:

```
? for(n=1,500,if(ispal(n) && ispal(2*n+1),print(n"\t\t"2*n+1)))
1               3
2               5
3               7
4               9
5               11
55              111
151             303
161             323
171             343
181             363
191             383
252             505
262             525
272             545
282             565
292             585
353             707
363             727
373             747
383             767
393             787
454             909
464             929
```

Nice.

Now I shall prove that these types of numbers are infinite.

Get ready for an ultra-sophisticated mind-melting proof coming your way.

Statement: There are infinitely many palindromes PAL such that 2*PAL+1 is also palindromic.

Proof: Let's take the two palindromes 494 and 363 as examples. Notice they have an undulating *aba* pattern. If we continue that pattern, always ending with an *a*, such as in *ababa...* or *ababababababa...* then we can always multiply those numbers by 2 and add 1 to obtain another palindrome. **Q.E.D.**

Examine these calculations for further clarification:

```
) gp > 49494*2+1
98989
) gp > 494*2+1
989
) gp > 4949494*2+1
9898989
) gp > 363*2+1
727
) gp > 36363*2+1
72727
```

Yes! I finally managed to put a proof in this book! Pretty trivial, but I'll take it. How do you like it now, gentleman? as Hemingway used to say.

Furthermore, it's also easy to see that if we take repeating fives: 5, 55, 555, 5555, ..., then double them and add one they will always produce repeating ones (repunits): 1, 11, 111, 1111, ... which are also (uninteresting and trivial) palindromes.

Here are some larger solutions I found:

```
4907094        9814189
4908094        9816189
4909094        9818189
4915194        9830389
4916194        9832389
4917194        9834389
4918194        9836389
4919194        9838389
4925294        9850589
4926294        9852589
4927294        9854589
4928294        9856589
4929294        9858589
4935394        9870789
4936394        9872789
4937394        9874789
4938394        9876789
4939394        9878789
4945494        9890989
4946494        9892989
4947494        9894989
4948494        9896989
4949494        9898989
5555555        11111111
```

While watching the numbers glide by on my screen, I noticed there would be quite a few solutions arriving, then they would stall for a significant period of time (probably due to them requiring a certain amount of digits to be solutions or something simple like that).

The largest ones I found were these (although I didn't try especially hard to find larger solutions):

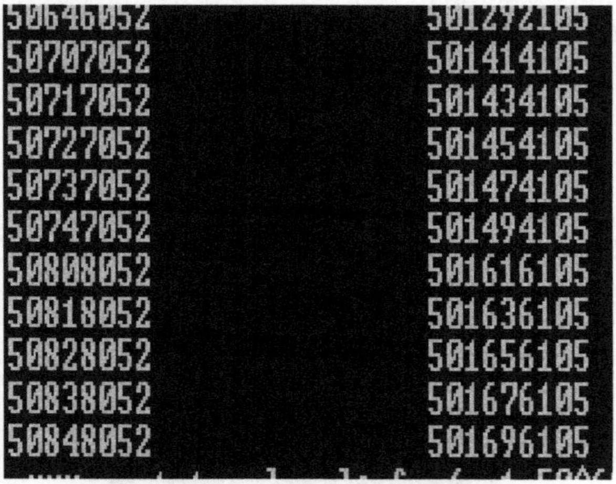

A Cautionary Tale on Collaboration

Many years ago I corresponded with a mathematician. He worked as an engineer for an oil company in another country. We were sending number theory problems and results back and forth, trying to work up decent material to submit to web sites and/or print journals. At this time in my life, I was addicted to doing computational number theory and submitting results to various web sites that I liked. Although I wasn't getting paid for it, this activity was a great learning experience for me (and tremendous fun).

Soon after the correspondence began with the mathematician, I had to prepare to get married to a wonderful woman I had been dating for a couple of years. After the marriage, we would of course be going on a nice honeymoon, which meant I would be away from a computer for a fairly long stretch of time. I didn't want to have to stop doing math and number theory work during this period, but I had no choice in the matter.

The mathematician kept sending me his results and ideas and soon it turned into a full on blitzkrieg/barrage of mathematical information that I couldn't keep up with. I tried telling him I was going to be getting married soon and wouldn't be able to respond to his emails for quite some time, but he continued sending his deluge of results day after day.

So the time came for my marriage and honeymoon. I was worried about all the time passing when I wouldn't be able to do any number theory computations or send in any results to math web sites (this was before the extremely powerful smart-phones we have today); it was such a habit ingrained in me (perhaps even an addiction) that I didn't want to just quit cold turkey.

While away for the wedding, occasionally I would gain access to a computer and check my usual math sites to see what other people were submitting. I noticed the mathematician I had been corresponding with was regularly sending in his results and some were those that he and I had worked on; he was listing me as co-author, which was fine with me. It was great seeing this because even though I had been traveling for the wedding and honeymoon it looked like I was still at home working diligently and submitting math results.

But then a problem developed. The mathematician continued sending in his work to sites and listing me as co-author, *except that I had never once laid eyes on the material he was submitting with **my name** on it.*

Uh-oh. What was I supposed to do? I remember seeing my name on a math sequence and thinking, "Wait a minute, I never worked on that. I haven't even seen this problem before. I would have definitely remembered doing computations and exploring any problem he suggested. What is he doing? Did he get confused as to what he had sent me?"

I guess among the barrage of math results he was emailing me, he eventually lost track as to what exactly I had worked on and what I had never seen. I didn't want to get credit for something that I had not contributed to. I should have emailed him about it, but with unreliable access to the internet while traveling, I didn't want to be distracted with trying to get the problem straightened out, which would have ruined my honeymoon due to being stressed out that I could not get to a computer regularly to straighten out the mess.

Then I noticed there were mistakes in some of the material he was submitting with my name on it. **Damn.** With my own math work, I would always *double and triple check my results* to make sure it was **absolutely 100% correct** before submitting anything to a web site. I definitely did not like someone sending in faulty material in my name and jeopardizing my math reputation.

Next, an editor of one of the web sites contacted me about some of the material listing me as co-author when it had a mistake, and I had to tell him: "I did work with this mathematician on a few things, but I noticed lately he has been submitting material listing me as co-author and I have never even seen it before. I don't know why he is still giving me credit for things when I don't deserve it. He must have just gotten confused as to what I had helped him with and what I had not."

The upside to this incident was that I had been worried about not being able to work during my wedding and honeymoon and was slightly disappointed that my math productivity would be falling off during this time, yet number theory results with my name on them were pouring into a web site when I was actually nowhere near a computer. It was kind of ironic and humorous to me.

But the downside was that I was being given credit for things I hadn't worked on and some of the results were filled with mistakes. My reputation could have easily gone down the drain fast. But finally the "co-authorship" stopped and I don't believe too much damage was sustained.

In the end, the moral of this story is that if you ever collaborate with someone, (on anything, not just math), make sure you get a final say-so on what is being submitted with your name on it.

Smarandache Car Primes

[This chapter is an excerpt from my book Mathematical Bliss]

In Smarandache Sequences Vol. I at the Smarandache web site[1], item #12 is a "Smarandache car" in which the figure of a vehicle can be seen as a picture outlined in a block of digits. In this note I report on primes that were found using the "Smarandache car" as the initial segment of their decimal expansions.

Numbers that enjoy certain properties such as primality

and that also contain a strong visual component is a concept closely related – in my mind at least – to that of "concrete poetry." Poems dubbed "concrete" are those in which the typographical arrangement of words or symbols plays a direct role in conveying the "meaning" of the poem[2]. A famous example is George Herbert's (1593-1633) poem "Easter Wings" in which its two stanzas are wing-shaped[3].

Regarding "concrete mathematics" (which is what I am defining here), there is of course no meaning to relate in the numbers presented. However, there is an element of humor in finding primes that have the figure of a vehicle pictured in their digits when they are formatted in a certain way. Hence this is a rather lighthearted math note, but nevertheless we offer the following primes and present a conjecture.

Below you will find the first Smarandache car prime (apologies that it does not resemble a Bugatti in shape):

```
111111111111111111111111111111111111111111111111111111111111111111
000000000000000000000000000000000000000000000000000000000000000000
000000000000000000111111111111111111111111100000000000000000000000
000000000000000001111111111111111111111111110000000000000000000000
000000000000000011000000000000000000000000011000000000000000000000
000000000000000110000000000000000000000000000110000000000000000000
000000011111111100000000000000000000000000000111111111111110000000
000000111111111000000000000000000000000000000011111111111111000000
000000110000000000000000000000000000000000000000000000000011200000
000000110000000000000000000000000000000000000000000000000011000000
000000110000044400000000000000000000000000000000000044400011000000
000000111111444441111111111111111111111111111111111444441111200000
000000011114444444111111111111111111111111111111114444444110000000
000000000000444440000000000000000000000000000000000444440000000000
000000000000044400000000000000000000000000000000000044400000000000
000000000000000000000000000000000000000000000000000000000000000000
000000000000000000000000000000000000000000000000000000000000000000
000000000000000000000000000000000000000000000000000000000000000000
000000000000000000000000000000000000000000000000000000000000000000
000000000000000000000000000000000000000000000000000000000000000000
000000000000000000000000000000000000000000000000000000000000000000
                000000000000000000000000000000000001
```

Notice the row of 1s placed along the top of the Smarandache car figure, which makes it different from the original image seen in [1]. Also the digits outlining the car have been bolded.

This prime was found by treating the picture of the Smarandache car as an integer, Z, then testing $Z * 10^n + 1$ for primality using the freely available PFGW program[4]. The values of n that make $Z * 10^n + 1$ prime are 300, 307, 313, 1511, and 1836, with no more terms up to 4500. The motivation behind multiplying Z by $10^n + 1$ was that the addition of zeros and a 1 would enable any probable prime P to be easily provable if at least 33% of P−1 could be factored. In other words, we hoped to give P−1 enough 2s and 5s to make it easily provable. Yet the first three values found: 300, 307, 313, did not allow Z * 10^n to have enough small factors and so they had to be certified with the online ECM factorization applet written by Dario Alpern[5]. The other two primes were easily provable since more than 33% of P−1 could be factored.

Conjecture: There are infinitely many Smarandache car primes.

Questions: What other "concrete" numerical figures can you design that simultaneously have mathematical properties? Can any squares, perfect powers, or Niven numbers be found that display "pictures" of any kind in their digits?

References

1. Smarandache Sequences, Vol. I, http://www.gallup.unm.edu/~smarandache/SNAQINT.txt

2. Wikipedia, "Concrete Poetry," http://en.wikipedia.org/wiki/Concrete_poetry

3. RPO, George Herbert, "Easter Wings", http://eir.library.utoronto.ca/rpo/display/poem973.html

4. PrimeFormGW (PFGW), Primality-Testing Program Discussion Group, http://groups.yahoo.com/group/primeform/

5. Dario Alpern, Factorization Using the Elliptic Curve Method Applet, http://www.alpertron.com.ar/ECM.HTM

On the Distribution of Harshad Numbers

A129287 Number of Harshad numbers between 10^n and 10^n + 100.

29, 30, 31, 29, 30, 28, 29, 30, 30, 29, 28, 28, 29, 30, 30, 29, 29, 28, 30, 30, 31, 29, 29, 28, 29, 30, 30, 29, 28, 28, 29, 30, 31, 29, 29, 28, 30, 30, 30, 29, 29, 28, 29, 30, 30, 29, 28, 28, 30, 30, 31, 29, 29, 28, 29, 30, 30, 29, 29, 28, 29, 30, 30, 29, 29, 28, 30, 30, 31 (list; graph; refs; listen; history; text; internal format)

OFFSET 3,1

COMMENTS Will every term be between 28 and 31 inclusive?

REFERENCES J. Earls, Red Zen, Lulu Press, NY, 2006, pp. 145 - 146. ISBN: 978-1-4303-2017-3.

LINKS Table of n, a(n) for n=3..71.

EXAMPLE There are exactly 29 Harshad numbers between 1000 and 1100, so the first term is 29.

CROSSREFS Cf. A005349.
Sequence in context: A210267 A210309 A165850 * A007642 A022399 A042694
Adjacent sequences: A129284 A129285 A129286 * A129288 A129289 A129290

KEYWORD nonn,base

AUTHOR Jason Earls (zevi_35711(AT)yahoo.com), May 26 2007

When you think about Harshad numbers (those that are divisible by the sum of their own digits; also called Niven numbers) as related to the sequence above and the small section of numbers it deals with (the interval of 100 at the tail end of successive powers of ten), it is not too surprising that all terms seem to be between 28 and 31 inclusive (for all terms up to n=2500 this is indeed the case, checked via computation). Let's do some more computations to see exactly what is going on here.

Comparing the two sequences produced for 10^5 and 10^6 powers (mod 100) we can examine what is happening more clearly:

```
(05:18) gp > for(n=10^5,10^5+100,if(isniv(n),print1(n%100", ")))
0, 2, 8, 10, 11, 12, 14, 16, 17, 20, 26, 32, 35, 40, 44, 48, 50, 51, 53, 56, 58,
 62, 71, 79, 80, 90, 92, 95, 96, 98, 0,
(05:18) gp > for(n=10^6,10^6+100,if(isniv(n),print1(n%100", ")))
0, 2, 6, 8, 10, 11, 12, 14, 16, 17, 20, 26, 32, 35, 40, 44, 50, 53, 56, 62, 71,
76, 80, 90, 92, 95, 96, 98, 0,
```

The 10^5 sequence has more solutions. A term missing from the 10^6 sequence is 48 and here is why: 100048 is divisible by 13 and 1000048 is not. Simple enough. Thus far it seems the problem boils down to simply studying various moduli as prime divisors. But let's examine some more data before jumping to any conclusions. Here are two other sequences to compare (I just picked powers of 208 and 209 at random):

```
(05:30) gp > for(n=10^208,10^208+100,if(isniv(n),print1(n%100", ")))
0, 2, 8, 10, 11, 12, 14, 16, 17, 20, 24, 26, 32, 35, 40, 44, 50, 53, 56, 62, 71,
 75, 80, 90, 92, 94, 95, 96, 98, 0,
(05:34) gp > for(n=10^209,10^209+100,if(isniv(n),print1(n%100", ")))
0, 2, 8, 10, 11, 12, 14, 16, 17, 20, 26, 32, 35, 40, 44, 48, 50, 51, 53, 56, 58,
 62, 71, 80, 90, 92, 95, 96, 98, 0,
```

The first term not shared by both is 24 and thus it turns out $10^{208}+24$ is divisible by 7 but $10^{209}+24$ is not. Makes sense so far.

Here are a few more sequences to contemplate:

```
(05:38) gp > for(n=10^5216,10^5216+100,if(isniv(n),print1(n%100", ")))
0, 2, 8, 10, 11, 12, 14, 16, 17, 20, 26, 32, 33, 35, 40, 44, 50, 53, 56, 62, 71,
 80, 90, 92, 95, 96, 98, 0,
(05:48) gp > for(n=10^5217,10^5217+100,if(isniv(n),print1(n%100", ")))
0, 2, 8, 10, 11, 12, 14, 15, 16, 17, 20, 26, 32, 35, 40, 44, 50, 53, 56, 62, 66,
 71, 80, 90, 92, 95, 96, 98, 0,
(05:49) gp > for(n=10^8888,10^8888+100,if(isniv(n),print1(n%100", ")))
0, 2, 8, 10, 11, 12, 14, 16, 17, 20, 26, 32, 33, 35, 40, 44, 50, 53, 56, 62, 71,
 80, 90, 92, 95, 96, 98, 0,
(05:50) gp > for(n=10^8889,10^8889+100,if(isniv(n),print1(n%100", ")))
0, 2, 8, 10, 11, 12, 14, 15, 16, 17, 20, 26, 32, 35, 40, 44, 50, 53, 56, 62, 66,
 71, 80, 90, 92, 95, 96, 98, 0,
```

So it's apparent that certain values are showing up (seemingly) all the time, with only occasional appearances by other values. Obviously a few simple rules of divisibility are at work here which guarantees that some values will always occur (the sum of digits being divisible by 3 rule; and even numbers divisible by 2 – i.e. numbers of the form 10^n+10 will always occur, etc.), but other values will not follow these elementary rules of divisibility and (perhaps) only show up due to certain (more rare) modulus reasons.

So now it seems like a good time to make a “Master List” of all 31 possible values, then gradually whittle the list down until it's easily seen why our main Harshad sequence at the beginning of this chapter always has between 28 and 31 terms inclusive. First we need to work on building the 31 terms of all possible solutions and then reduce them through divisibility and modulus arguments. (This will not generate a rigorous proof of course, but only give some basic reasons for the 28-31 inclusive criteria.)

To reiterate, our method below will be to create a "Master List" and gradually reduce it down via computation to prove the number of Harshads occurring at trailing powers of one hundred for powers of 10 will always be between 28 and 31 inclusive (still sounds confusing, but you'll realize the method soon enough).

Through computational experimentation, this Master List was determined:

MASTER LIST (31 values):
0, 2, 8, 10, 11, 12, 14, 15, 16, 17, 20, 24, 26, 32, 35, 40, 44, 50, 53, 56, 62, 66, 71, 75, 80, 90, 92, 94, 95, 96, 98.

(What can we say about terms like 3 and 7 not appearing? In the case of 3, it's because for numbers of the form 10^n+3 the smallest prime factor will always be at least 7 or higher (I think, I can't really prove that). As for other values, I have not looked into them, so others may in fact exist, which is why we are not proving anything rigorous in this chapter, but only offering some general rules of what might be occurring.)

Let's get started reducing our Master List, i.e. eliminating the ones that obviously have a reason for always showing up, and trying to find a few wild-card values that do not have a legitimate reason for being on the list (if any in fact do exist).

First, we shall determine which terms of the sequence of Harshads between 10^n and 10^n+100 are such that their digital sum is divisible by 3, which are these:

2, 8, 11, 14, 17, 20, 26, 32, 35, 44, 50, 53, 56, 62, 71, 80, 92, 95, 98.

This reduces our list significantly!

REDUCED MASTER LIST (now only 12 values!):
0, 10, 12, 15, 16, 24, 40, 66, 75, 90, 94, 96.

Next are those that have the simple divisibility by 2 rule (I had to locate three or four different types of solution sequences to determine all of the possible values):
0, 2, 6, 8, 10, 12, 14, 16, 20, 24, 26, 32, 40, 44, 50, 56, 62, 66, 76, 80, 90, 92, 94, 96, 98.

REDUCED MASTER LIST
15, 75.

Now only 2 values left, wow! That was fast!

So now all we have left is to determine under what conditions the 15 and 75 solutions will occur and we have eliminated all the values in our Master List with no wild-cards appearing. Will that be a proof that the terms will always be between 28 and 31 inclusive in the original sequence? No, it won't be fully rigorous because we haven't ruled out other values (not on our Master List) from possibly occurring.

Oh man. After searching for solutions other than evens and those not divisible by 3, other solutions popped up that were not on our original Master List!

Observe:

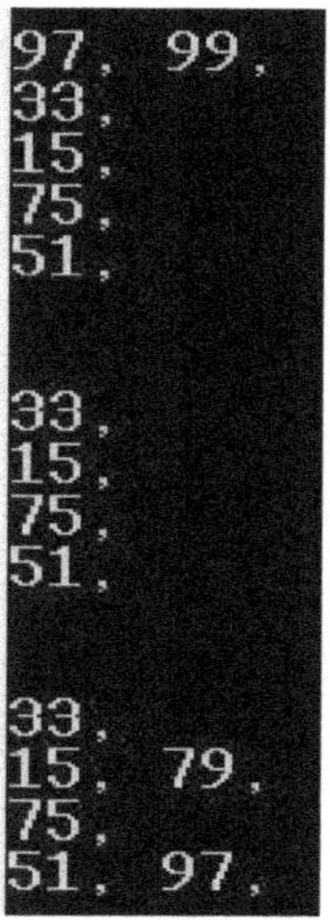

Where the hell did those come from? Here is our original Master List:

MASTER LIST (all possible solutions, 31 values):
0, 2, 8, 10, 11, 12, 14, 15, 16, 17, 20, 24, 26, 32, 35, 40, 44, 50, 53, 56, 62, 66, 71, 75, 80, 90, 92, 94, 95, 96, 98.

As you can see, 33, 51, 79, 97, and 99 were not on the list. How could that happen? I will have to think about this some more... Screw it, let's just add those values to our reduced list and see if we can eliminate them.

UPDATED MASTER LIST (now 7 values):
15, 33, 51, 75, 79, 97, 99.

After running more computations, I determined that when the exponent *m* is of the form 3, 9, 15, 21, ...

(6*n+3) then 10^m+15 will be divisible by 7; also when the exponent m is of the form 2, 8, 14, 20, 26, ... (6*n+2) then 10^m+33 will also be divisible by 7; and when exponent m is of the form 5, 11, 17, 23, 29, ... (3*n-1) then 10^m+51 will be divisible by 7; these eliminate the first three values on our Updated Master List.

NEW UPDATED MASTER LIST:
75, 79, 97, 99.

What next? More basic modulus arguments: when the exponent is of the form 4, 10, 16, 22, 28, ... (6*n+4) then 10^m+75 will be divisible by 13. When exponent is 5, 21, 37, 53, 69, 85, 101, (16*n-27) for n>=2, then 10^m+79 will be divisible by 17. When m is of the form 23, 39, 55, 71, 87, then 10^m+97 will be divisible by 17. And when m is of the form 25, 43, 61, 79, 97, then 10^m+99 will be divisible by 19. That covers them all.

Hence that is why in the sequence of the amount of Harshad numbers between 10^n and 10^n+100 they will always be between 28 and 31 inclusive. Wrong, that isn't a rigorous proof. Theoretically someone may be able to compute solutions that we have not yet seen in this chapter. Regardless, I provided some modulus arguments to give a general outline of why our original sequence always seems to be between 28 and 31 inclusive.

Questions:

Can you find a solution that was not given in this chapter? Will the amount of Harshad numbers between

10^n and 10^n+1000 always be between 186 and 203 inclusive? (See sequence below):

for(n=4,400,print1(harshct(n)","))
200,192,201,188,202,189,197,191,202,189,200,188,201,
191,200,187,198,191,199,191,200,189,201,189,198,190,
203,188,201,190,200,191,198,188,201,190,200,190,198,
189,200,189,199,191,203,188,200,189,200,192,200,188,
200,189,197,191,201,189,203,188,198,191,200,188,200,
192,201,190,199,186,199,190,199,192,202,188,201,189,
199,191,202,189,200,190,198,189,198,189,200,189,200,
190,202,189,201,190,199,192,201,188,...

The Sopfr(n) Earls Conjecture

[This chapter is an excerpt from my book Mathematical Bliss]

The integers 714 and 715 are known as "Ruth-Aaron" pairs because they are consecutive numbers whose sum of prime factors are both equal to each other. For example,

$$714 = 2*3*7*17$$
$$715 = 5*11*13$$
and
$$2+3+7+17 = 29 = 5+11+13$$

The Ruth-Aaron part of the name comes from Hank Aaron breaking the home run record in April of 1974 with his 715th home run, which was previously held by Babe Ruth who had 714 home runs.

If we let sopfr(n) be the sum of prime factors of n (counting multiplicity), then we can see that Ruth-Aaron pairs are numbers satisfying the equation

$$\mathrm{sopfr}(n) = \mathrm{sopfr}(n+1)$$

Here are all of the Ruth-Aaron pairs up to 10^5:

```
? for(n=1,100000,if(sopfr(n)==sopfr(n+1),print1(n":"n+1",")))
5:6,8:9,15:16,77:78,125:126,714:715,948:949,1330:1331,1520:1521,1862:1863,2491:2
492,3248:3249,4185:4186,4191:4192,5405:5406,5560:5561,5959:5960,6867:6868,8280:8
281,8463:8464,10647:10648,12351:12352,14587:14588,16932:16933,17080:17081,18490:
18491,20450:20451,24895:24896,26642:26643,26649:26650,28448:28449,28809:28810,33
019:33020,37828:37829,37881:37882,41261:41262,42624:42625,43215:43216,44831:4483
2,44891:44892,47544:47545,49240:49241,52554:52555,53192:53193,57075:57076,63344:
63345,63426:63427,68264:68265,68949:68950,70356:70357,72500:72501,81175:81176,89
979:89980,95709:95710,98119:98120,98644:98645,99163:99164,
```

After reading about Ruth-Aaron pairs and finding many of them, I became curious about numbers satisfying sopfr(n) = sopfr(n+2) and easily found an abundance of solutions. Next I tried sopfr(n) = sopfr(n+3) and again had no trouble finding solutions – (my computer was spitting them out one after the other and at the time I had an extremely weak, ghetto-computer).

Hence it seemed to me that no matter what amount I added to the right side of the equation, I always seemed to find a solution. Here are solutions for sopfr(n) = sopfr(n+20) for example:

```
(15:26) gp > for(n=1,100000,if(sopfr(n)==sopfr(n+20),print1(n":"n+20",")))
28:48,100:120,105:125,160:180,300:320,456:476,1540:1560,2125:2145,2500:2520,3484
:3504,4408:4428,4655:4675,6588:6608,6916:6936,7987:8007,9342:9362,13447:13467,14
280:14300,17205:17225,18960:18980,26600:26620,26818:26838,27448:27468,30400:3042
0,30855:30875,35136:35156,36666:36686,37240:37260,45175:45195,46364:46384,46813:
46833,47104:47124,47575:47595,49820:49840,55314:55334,59055:59075,60151:60171,64
505:64525,64960:64980,73186:73206,78864:78884,83700:83720,83820:83840,92415:9243
5,92466:92486,93112:93132,93150:93170,
```

After running many more tests in which I chose different

k values at random, I eventually conjectured that–

For any *k* there is always at least one *n* value such that sopfr(n) =sopfr(n + k).

(The conjecture also seems to hold for sopf(n), the sum of prime factors of *n*, not counting multiplicity.)

I sent my conjecture to Carlos Rivera's *Prime Puzzles & Problems* web site where he soon featured it as a puzzle. People wrote in with ideas for proofs but no one ever found a sufficiently rigorous demonstration; and to this day my conjecture still stands.

Perhaps you would like to devote the rest of your life to proving the Earls Conjecture that for any value of *k* there is always at least one *n* such that sopfr(n) = sopfr(n + k)? I can't think of a better way for you to spend your time.

Digit Concrete Prime

```
999999999999999999999999999999999999999999999999999999
900000000000000000000000000000000000000000000000000009
900888888000008888880000888888000088888800088888888009
900880008880000088000008800008800000880000000088000009
900880000880000088000008800000000000880000000088000009
900880000880000088000008800000000000880000000088000009
900880000880000088000008800888000000880000000088000009
900880000880000088000008800008800000880000000088000009
900880008800000088000008800008800000880000000088000009
900888888000008888880000888888000088888800000088000009
900000000000000000000000000000000000000000000000000009
999999999999999999999999999999999999999999999999999999
                   000000000000001
```

Pick a numeral from 0 to 9. Those are digits. And decimal digits do so much for us in this incredible world. They are the basic symbols of our modern system of numeration.

Cypher, nought. Ace, unity. Drop a deuce, motherfreaker.

Digit hunters are looked down upon in our modern world of mathematics. But the digits making up our numbers are so important a few people become intrigued and infatuated with them for their own sake. I don't blame them.

Tercet, ternion, terzetto, triad, troika. Trip on out, math nerds.

Mathematics would be nowhere without the humble yet

mighty digit.

Quadruplet, quarternion. Fivesome, pentad, quintuplet. Hexad, sixer. Heptad, septet. Sex it on up.

Decimal digits are indeed super-incredible objects.

Octad, ogdoad. Ennead, niner. Egghead phone home.

I have been in love with digits all my life.

Notice the concrete prime at the beginning of this chapter; it spells out "**DIGIT**" in its decimal expansion. Hopefully the letters can be seen clearly by the reader. This prime is a tribute to the incredible mathematical entities that make up our modern system of numbers.

The **DIGIT** prime above is an example of what I like to call "concrete mathematics" since the concept (in my opinion) is very similar to concrete poetry (poems in which the typographical arrangement of symbols or words plays a direct role in conveying the "meaning" of a poem). But where concrete math differs from concrete poetry is that it deals primarily with classes of numbers (primes, squares, triangulars, harshads, etc.) that possess a certain visual component when the digits are arranged in a certain way – i.e. the digits are "formatted" in rows so that a word, phrase, or image can be "pictured" in the decimal expansion. (Remember that the definition of a prime number is an integer without any divisors except for itself and one. For example, 2, 3, 5, 7, 11, 13, ... are all prime numbers.)

Notice the string: "0000000000000001" at the very end of the **DIGIT** prime given above. This "mathematical extension" if you will (which can also be written more compactly as "*10^16+1") is absolutely necessary for the number to be prime, since basically I am treating the large main block of digits (ending with the long bottom string of 9s) with "DIGIT" spelled out in the decimal expansion as a constant (let's call it D) in a polynomial that I then run a search on to hopefully find a prime value for D*10^*n*+1. Usually I prefer that the exponent value be small enough so I can simply list all the digits in one complete "block" (which I did with the DIGIT prime above) and not have to resort to putting in the "*10^*n*+*x*" value at the end (as I have to do with other primes), which I feel does not properly represent the prime since it slightly ruins the lack of simplicity and symmetry that can be achieved by listing all the necessary digits in one large chunk; adding the mathematical extension at the end causes the prime to lose a little of its special character and charm – but there's really nothing I can do about that. My job is to merely hunt for the specific concrete prime and accept whatever pops up.

Usually the concrete primes I find will have more prime values associated with them than the main one listed at the beginning of this chapter (see my book *Concrete Calculator-Word Primes* for many examples). And for the **DIGIT** prime this was also the case: others with the same **DIGIT** decimal expansion but with different digits at the end are: **D*10^16+1**; **D*10^388+1**; and **D*10^622+1**; perhaps the reader would like to compute their decimal expansions and have fun formatting them like the **DIGIT** prime given at the beginning of this chapter (and the one at the end.) Keep in mind, the formatting of the **DIGIT** concrete prime is very important. Here is what it looks like in an un-formatted state:

9999999999999999999999999999999999999999999990
0000000000000000000000000000000000000000000099
00008888000088888888008888880008888888880099
00088008800088000000000000880000880000000009
900880000880088000000000000880000880000000000
9900880000880088888880000088000000088800000
99008800008800880000000000088000000000888000
9900880000880088000000000000880000000000880
09900088008800088000000000008800000000000880
0099000088880000888888800888888008888888880
0099000000000000000000000000000000000000000
0009999999999999999999999999999999999999999999
990000000000000000000000000000000001

Not especially pulchritudinous, is it? Yet it's still amazing to me that out of all those 8s, 0s, 9s, and a 1, an actual "word" came be conjured up through simple formatting that represents one of the greatest mathematical concepts of all time.

Another **DIGIT** prime is this one (notice the large "*10^622+1" extension at the end) except you will have to replace the periods below with zeros to make it a legitimate prime ready to be tested by your favorite prime-testing software:

```
999999999999999999999999999999999999999999999999999999
9....................................................9
9..888888.....888888....888888....888888...88888888..9
9..88...888.....88.....88....88.....88........88.....9
9..88....88.....88.....88...........88........88.....9
9..88....88.....88.....88...........88........88.....9
9..88....88.....88.....88..888......88........88.....9
9..88....88.....88.....88....88.....88........88.....9
9..88...88......88.....88....88.....88........88.....9
9..888888.....888888....888888....888888......88.....9
9....................................................9
999999999999999999999999999999999999999999999999999999
                    *10^622+1
```

Questions

1. Can you construct your own concrete **DIGIT** decimal expansion (different from the one in this chapter) to find some **DIGIT** concrete primes of your own?

2. Can you find another form of number (perhaps square, harshad, or triangular) that has the name "**DIGIT**" pictured somewhere in its digits?

A Challenge for Mrs. Thornburgette

Mrs. Thornburgette was a wonderful college algebra teacher, although she was a rather strange person. She was about 45, tall and thin with angular facial features, and bright pale-green eyes that pierced your soul if you gazed into them long enough. Her skin was light yellow due to her rather unhealthy diet of Coca-Cola and sugar cookies while barely consuming any meat or vegetables. She lost her temper occasionally if she became frustrated while working a certain algebra problem on the board, but she could be very encouraging to students that showed the right amount of mathematical talent. When she became really excited, she had a terrible habit of cursing uncontrollably – we suspected she suffered from a mild case of Tourette's Syndrome.

Mrs. Thornburgette also had a strange habit of arranging her hair. She wore sort of a long yellow mullet hairdo with big spiked bangs on top, and every few minutes she had an unconscious habit of running her slim fingers down the length of her thin scraggly hair in the back to straighten it, then she would bring her hands up to the very top of her head and scratch into her bangs very hard, really digging in with her fingertips, to make the bangs stand up taller and to create sort of a fashionable messy look.

One day late in the afternoon Mrs. Thornburgette was teaching us how to do matrix algebra multiplication, and she was working an extremely long problem on the board. She had been working theses types of problems all day long for her different classes, and if you have ever worked a big matrix multiplication problem, you know that if you make one teeny-tiny mistake, the whole problem will be wrong, which can be a real disaster if you have spent thirty to forty-five minutes doing many consecutive multiplications, trying to keep track of every single little answer along the way, only to end up with the wrong answer in the end.

Mrs. Thornburgette was getting progressively frustrated working each of the matrix multiplication problems. She had gotten several wrong answers throughout the day after spending too much time on each one, and when the big muscular football players would laugh at her mistakes from the back of the room, she would become extremely pissed-off.

For our class, she worked another problem and ended up with the wrong answer, in fact it was a pretty far off from the correct one, which we looked up in the back of the book. Yarborough Johnson, the local star running back on the football team guffawed loudly when he heard Mrs. Thornburgette display her disgust at getting another answer different from the one listed in the back of the book.

Mrs. Thornburgette heard Yarborough laugh and finally she'd had enough. She threw down her marker and strolled toward Yarborough Johnson who was sitting at the back of the room.

“Would you like to make any comments on this problem, Mr. Johnson?” asked Mrs. Thornburgette.

“Nope, *hee-hee-hee*,” snickered Yarborough.

“Well, I think I am going to have *you* work the next problem to show us all how it's done. Go on up to the board my dear Yarborough, and we'll see what you can do.”

“No, thanks,” he said, smiling to display a row of pure white perfectly straight teeth.

“What?” She folded her arms in front of her lean body, she was so mad that her unhealthy skin looked even more yellow.

“I said I'm not going to work the problem, Mrs. Thornburgette.”

“Oh yes, you will, or you will flunk my fucking... uh, excuse me, you will fail my class,” she said, trying to cover up her Tourette's slip of cursing.

He smiled again, raising his head slightly, and the veins in his muscular weightlifting neck bristled. “Well, how about if I show the class something else?”

“And just what might that be, sir?”

Yarborough rose from his desk, carrying his smart-phone with him. He strolled boldly over to the projection machine, his stout 220 lb physique moving with supreme confidence, where he leaned down and flipped on the projector, then he took a cord and plugged it into his smart phone. He started tapping away quickly and soon in front of the other students the projection machine flashed this large image for all the class to observe:

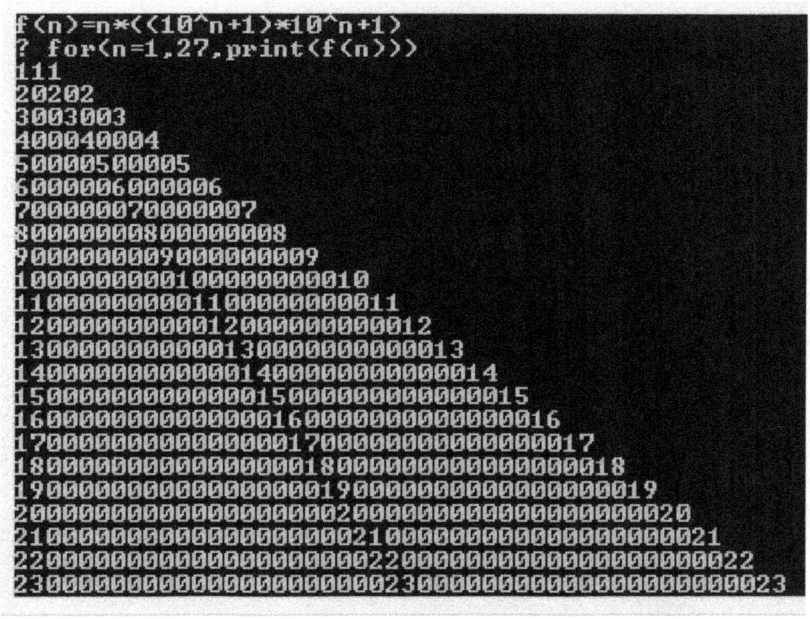

```
f(n)=n*((10^n+1)*10^n+1)
? for(n=1,27,print(f(n)))
111
20202
3003003
400040004
50000500005
6000006000006
700000070000007
80000000800000008
9000000009000000009
1000000000100000000010
110000000001100000000011
12000000000012000000000012
1300000000000130000000000013
140000000000001400000000000014
15000000000000015000000000000015
1600000000000000160000000000000016
170000000000000001700000000000000017
18000000000000000018000000000000000018
1900000000000000000190000000000000000019
200000000000000000002000000000000000000020
21000000000000000000021000000000000000000021
2200000000000000000000220000000000000000000022
230000000000000000000002300000000000000000000023
```

"This function, f(*n*)=*n**((10^*n*+1)*10^*n*+1) produces a striking stack of numbers," Yarborough said in a deep authoritative voice.

Mrs. Thornburgette sat down in Yarborough's chair, her mouth slightly open and her eyes wide.

"Can we discover any interesting properties in this stack of numbers?" Yarborough asked.

The class remained dead silent.

"First off, none will ever be prime since the odd indexed terms will always have a factor of 3, while the even indexed terms will always have a factor of 2. Can anyone rigorously prove this statement?"

The class did not respond.

Yarborough leaned down and tapped on his smart-phone for several seconds. "Now, let's examine the prime factors of these numbers and see what they might tell us."

```
? for(n=1,1111,if(isprime(f(n)),print1(n",")))
? for(n=1,66,print(n":"factor(f(n))))
1:[3, 1; 37, 1]
2:[2, 1; 3, 1; 7, 1; 13, 1; 37, 1]
3:[3, 2; 333667, 1]
4:[2, 2; 3, 1; 7, 1; 13, 1; 37, 1; 9901, 1]
5:[3, 1; 5, 1; 31, 1; 37, 1; 2906161, 1]
6:[2, 1; 3, 2; 19, 1; 52579, 1; 333667, 1]
7:[3, 1; 7, 1; 37, 1; 43, 1; 1933, 1; 10838689, 1]
8:[2, 3; 3, 1; 7, 1; 13, 1; 37, 1; 9901, 1; 99990001, 1]
9:[3, 3; 757, 1; 440334654777631, 1]
10:[2, 1; 3, 1; 5, 1; 7, 1; 13, 1; 31, 1; 37, 1; 211, 1; 241, 1; 2161, 1; 290616
1, 1]
11:[3, 1; 11, 1; 37, 1; 67, 1; 134462821031329837 3, 1]
12:[2, 2; 3, 2; 19, 1; 52579, 1; 333667, 1; 999999000001, 1]
13:[3, 1; 13, 1; 37, 1; 900900900900990990990991, 1]
14:[2, 1; 3, 1; 7, 3; 13, 1; 37, 1; 43, 1; 127, 1; 1933, 1; 2689, 1; 459691, 1;
10838689, 1]
15:[3, 2; 5, 1; 238681, 1; 333667, 1; 4185502830133110721, 1]
16:[2, 4; 3, 1; 7, 1; 13, 1; 37, 1; 9901, 1; 99990001, 1; 9999999900000001, 1]
17:[3, 1; 17, 1; 37, 1; 613, 1; 210631, 1; 52986961, 1; 13168164561429877, 1]
18:[2, 1; 3, 3; 757, 1; 70541929, 1; 14175966169, 1; 440334654777631, 1]
19:[3, 1; 19, 1; 37, 1; 21319, 1; 10749631, 1; 3931123022305129377976519, 1]
20:[2, 2; 3, 1; 5, 1; 7, 1; 13, 1; 31, 1; 37, 1; 61, 1; 211, 1; 241, 1; 2161, 1;
 9901, 1; 2906161, 1; 4188901, 1; 39526741, 1]
```

The projector flashed the new image.

"It seems pretty messy, I know," said Yarborough. But look carefully at the factors of the 13th term.

```
13:[3, 1; 13, 1; 37, 1; 9009009009009909909909991, 1]
```

“Notice the strange digital pattern in the largest prime factor there. Isn't that amazing? The single nines with double zeroes, then the double nines with single zeroes, and a final one at the end. I love that. I can't believe prime numbers exist that display this kind of intriguing pattern.”

Yarborough looked at the back of the room to gauge Mrs. Thornburgette's interest in his problem. She was still sitting in his seat, but now her mouth was open even further while her eyes were open as far as they would go.

“Let's examine a few more prime factors of these numbers to see what we can find,” Yarborough continued.

```
641709400063151, 1]
26:[2, 1; 3, 1; 7, 1; 13, 3; 37, 1; 157, 1; 6397, 1; 216451, 1; 388847808493, 1;
 9009009009009909909909991, 1]
27:[3, 4; 163, 1; 9397, 1; 2462401, 1; 676421558270641, 1; 130654897808007778425
046117, 1]
28:[2, 2; 3, 1; 7, 3; 13, 1; 37, 1; 43, 1; 127, 1; 1933, 1; 2689, 1; 9901, 1; 22
6549, 1; 459691, 1; 10838689, 1; 44581922233203340849, 1]
29:[3, 1; 29, 1; 37, 1; 4003, 1; 72559, 1; 31017025165802975904515779323733394983
42763245483, 1]
30:[2, 1; 3, 2; 5, 1; 19, 1; 29611, 1; 52579, 1; 238681, 1; 333667, 1; 3762091,
1; 8985695684401, 1; 41855028301331110721, 1]
31:[3, 1; 31, 1; 37, 1; 900900900900900900900900900990990990990990990990990
0991, 1]
32:[2, 5; 3, 1; 7, 1; 13, 1; 37, 1; 97, 1; 9901, 1; 206209, 1; 99990001, 1; 6655
4101249, 1; 75118313082913, 1; 9999999900000001, 1]
33:[3, 2; 11, 1; 199, 1; 397, 1; 34849, 1; 333667, 1; 362853724342990469324766235
47426886978631188605388 3, 1]
34:[2, 1; 3, 1; 7, 1; 13, 1; 17, 1; 37, 1; 613, 1; 210631, 1; 52986961, 1; 29107
8844423, 1; 13168164561429877, 1; 377526955309799110357, 1]
35:[3, 1; 5, 1; 7, 1; 31, 1; 37, 1; 43, 1; 1933, 1; 2906161, 1; 10838689, 1; 307
03738801, 1; 625437743071, 1; 578020503087861919654O9441, 1]
36:[2, 2; 3, 3; 109, 1; 757, 1; 153469, 1; 70541929, 1; 14175966169, 1; 44033465
4777631, 1; 597795771563345338666548382 81, 1]
37:[3, 1; 37, 3; 3055705151864730 7, 1; 884598117086562911927199 7, 1; 9007781439 6
055017938257237117, 1]
```

“Notice on the screen the 26th and 31st terms also contain single nine double zero and double nine with single zero plus one prime factors. When I first computed this last night in my room at 2 AM, I felt like I'd made a major discovery in computational number theory. But soon you will see there is even more to my discovery. Before I reveal it however, I would like to see if Mrs. Thornburgette has any comments to make. Mrs. Thornburgette, you have the floor..."

She remained seated and shook her head back and forth, "I... uhh... I... damn... ummhhhh....."

She couldn't respond, so Yarborough Johnson continued his impromptu lecture.

"Here is my little challenge for you all, and especially for Mrs. Thornburgette. I have discovered a proof that primes of this form are infinite, and that they pop up as factors of this set of numbers infinitely often. I know my proof is correct. I emailed it to a mathematician at a university in California who had written papers with Paul Erdos and he confirmed its accuracy and high level of rigor. So my challenge is, anyone who can match my proof, or find another proof in a different form that's still completely accurate, I will pay them one thousand dollars of my own money. And don't worry, I'll know if you submit a faulty proof, my mathematician friend in California agreed to help me judge any proofs that are submitted."

The class gasped and looked around at each other. They all wanted a thousand dollars to buy drugs and alcohol with, but they had no fucking clue how to do proofs in number theory, or even what the proper definition of number theory was.

Mrs. Thornburgette rose and walked to the front of the class. She had finally gathered her composure enough to speak. “You can sit down now Mr. Yarborough Johnson.” She paused and did that thing with her hair, straightening it in back, then scrunching up her bangs.

Yarborough strutted back to his seat with his big arms cocked out, wearing a proud grin.

“Now that is what I'm fucking talking about,” Mrs. Thornburgette said, her Tourette's now in full swing. “Do you see what this motherfucker has accomplished?”

A girl with a bright red punk rock hairdo raised her hand.

“Yes, Melissa?” said Mrs. Thornburgette.

“Ma'am, do you realize you're cursing in front of the class?”

“I don't care, this is fucking amazing,” she was so excited now her Tourette's really went wild. “I'm so proud of Mr. Johnson for showing the class this goddamn number theory problem. I'm fucking thrilled he managed to work this out on his own and find these bitchin' solutions.”

She paused in her vulgar speech, put her hands on her hips, and glared out at the class with widened eyes, hoping her enthusiasm would truly register in their brains.

“What a presentation, this kid is fucking great,” she

continued. "Yarborough, I sincerely hope you continue on to one day do some serious fucking mathematics. Yes, these little visual number theory problems are nice, but you could go on to become a real hardcore bad-ass mathematician someday. I hope you stick with it. You seem to have some real fucking talent here for this kind of shit. Keep going with it son."

She glanced up to the projector screen where it was still retaining the last image of numbers that Yarborough had presented, even though he had now unplugged his smartphone and carried it off.

"Right on, Yarborough," she continued, barely aware of her unconscious Tourette's rant. "Look at those motherfucking numbers people, that shit is really nice. Ya know, you kids don't realize, sometimes I kneel down beside my bed at night and actually **PRAY** to **ALMIGHTY GOD** for **just one student** who is *truly hungry* for knowledge, a student who *really wants to learn* some fucking radical math facts. And usually I get no answer to my sincere prayers. But now Yarborough comes in here and blows my socks off with this goddamn number theory bullshit. It's amazing and inspiring. I don't think I can find a fucking proof for what he described. In fact, I'm positive I can't do it. That prime stuff is way beyond me. But maybe one of you little sons-of-bitches can. Who knows, I never expected Yarborough to do what he did today, so maybe one of you bright little dip-shits can pull off something amazing as well. Nevertheless, even if no one proves this sweet-ass problem and claims the goddamn thousand smackaroos, I'll never forget what this fucking bastard jock managed to show us here today."

Proper Divisor Summation Palindromes

Back in the very early days of number theory, mathematicians liked to pose challenge problems to one another.

They liked to kind of provoke each other into seeing if they would actually work on a number theory problem.

Because back then most people thought the field of number theory was sort of a trivial waste of time.

The problem below might prove that sentiment to be true.

A palindrome is a number that reads the same way forward and backward.

The sigma function sums the divisors of a number, including the number itself.

But we don't want the number itself.

Only the proper divisors.

So we'll use this function: s(n) = sigma(n) – n

Okay?

Keep the above statements in your mind as you consider this question:

Are there any squares such that when all of their proper divisors are summed the result is a palindrome?

Yup.

Consider the number 182^2= 33124. Summing its proper divisors produces the palindrome 39893 (I'll leave it to the reader to actually calculate and sum all the proper divisors of 33124).

Here are the values of n such that s(n^2) is a palindrome, where s(n) is the sum of proper divisors:

1, 2, 3, 5, 6, 7, 39, 43, 110, 182, 211, 241, 251, 271, 281, 433, 443, 463, 827, 857, 877, 887, 2111, 2221, 2441, 2551, 4003, 4663, 4993, 8117, 8447, 8887, 11929, 14199, 17264, 20101, 20201, 21011, 21211, 21611, 21911, 22621, 22721, 22921, 23131, 23431, 23531, 23831, 24841, 25951, 26161, 26261, 26561, 26861, 27271, 28081, 28181, 29191, 40903, 41113, 41213, 41413, 41513, 41813, 42023, 42223, 42323, 42923, 43133, 43633, 43933, 44543, 44843, 45053, 45553, 45853, 45953, 45991, 46663, 48383, 48883, 49193, 49393, 49993, 65001, 80107, 80207, 80407, 81017, 81517, 81817, ...

Most of the numbers above when squared have only 3 total divisors (including the number itself) and it's easy to see that when *n* is prime such that adding 1 to it will produce a palindrome, then it will be in the sequence above. Therefore the "interesting" terms of this sequence will be those having **more than** 3 total divisors.

Namely these:

```
<f(numdiv(n^2)>3&&is
36:9,
1521:9,
12100:27,
33124:27,
142301041:9,
201611601:9,
298045696:81,
2115172081:27,
4225130001:27,
49567233769:9,
59198296249:9,
72636718144:63,
413986722724:9,
772424781129:63,
1222705177600:99,
1502070848100:81,
```

Isn't it interesting that the square 1222705177600 has 99 divisors! Consider this data:

X = 1222705177600;

numberofdivisors(X) = 99

divisors(X) = [1, 2, 4, 5, 8, 10, 16, 20, 25, 32, 40, 50, 64, 80, 100, 128, 160, 200, 256, 320, 400, 512, 640, 800, 1024, 1280, 1600, 2560, 3200, 5120, 6400, 6911, 12800, 13822, 25600, 27644, 34555, 55288, 69110, 110576, 138220, 172775, 221152, 276440, 345550, 442304, 552880, 691100, 884608, 1105760, 1382200, 1769216, 2211520, 2764400, 3538432, 4423040, 5528800, 7076864, 8846080, 11057600, 17692160, 22115200, 35384320, 44230400, 47761921, 88460800, 95523842, 176921600, 191047684, 238809605, 382095368, 477619210, 764190736, 955238420, 1194048025, 1528381472, 1910476840, 2388096050, 3056762944, 3820953680, 4776192100, 6113525888, 7641907360, 9552384200, 12227051776, 15283814720, 19104768400, 24454103552, 30567629440, 38209536800, 48908207104, 61135258880, 76419073600, 122270517760, 152838147200, 244541035520, 305676294400, 611352588800, 1222705177600]

s(X) = 1808561658081 = palindrome

Conjecture: the sequence of squares such that their sum of proper divisors is a palindrome, and their total number of divisors is greater than 3, is infinite!

I hope you can embrace this problem wholeheartedly with much enthusiasm.

Send it to someone as a challenge problem.

Enjoy its wonderful attributes.

Try to prove the conjecture.

Thank you.

The Adrenaline Junkie

The adrenaline junkie loved leaping off of high skyscraper like objects or out of airplanes and parachuting down to the ground. He was addicted to the adrenaline rush he felt when jumping from something extremely high until he would deploy his parachute and float safely to the earth. Like most adrenaline junkies, he had a hard time recreating the rush of his very first jump, so he became addicted and needed to find a way to do some type of leap nearly every day.

The adrenaline junkie's favorite thing to do was pay a pilot to fly him up near the edge of the stratosphere where he would then jump out and feel the sensation of falling for a very long time. But pilots who could fly that high were extremely expensive, and the adrenaline junkie had an addiction to feed daily, which meant most of the time he had to settle for high buildings to leap from. The adrenaline junkie spent most of his time traveling to a nearby city where he would illegally climb and jump from a huge skyscraper. This activity was of course illegal but usually the adrenaline junkie could perform his stunt and get out of there before the police arrived.

Another activity the adrenaline junkie enjoyed was doing computational number theory. Yes, this is indeed a strange hobby for a parachutist, but during his free falls to earth, after the initial surge of adrenaline had subsided, the adrenaline junkie would become quite bored so he would take out his smart-phone and begin exploring various properties of numbers. He loved numbers of all kinds and felt a real thrill when investigating their "secrets." The adrenaline junkie loved *elementary* number theory above all; and often during his parachute descents, he would take out his smart phone and start working on a problem. He even felt small surges of adrenaline from time to time as he floated to the ground while engaging in computational number theory.

As he was floating down from a jump one fine day with the beautiful Oklahoma scenery displayed below him, the adrenaline junkie got an idea for a prime number sequence. He thought to himself: *I wonder if there is a number n such that if you multiply it by 100 and add 1 it's prime, and also if you multiply the same number by 1000 and add 1 it's prime, then if you multiply it by 10000 and add 1 it's also prime, and if you multiply it by 100000 and add 1 it's prime, and keep continuing like that... how far could we go and still find primes?*

The adrenaline junkie pulled out his smart-phone and began punching buttons until he had written out a simple little Pari script:

```
{ F(m) = for(n=1,m, if(isprime(100*n+1)
&& isprime(1000*n+1) && isprime(10000*n+1)
&& isprime(100000*n+1) &&
isprime(1000000*n+1) &&
isprime(10000000*n+1) &&
isprime(100000000*n+1), print1(n",")))) }
```

He pushed `[ENTER]` and after a few seconds solutions began popping up on his phone's screen:

241080, 3261538, 10612420, 11843265, 16062865, 22257627, 25108804, 26373004, ...

“Wow! It's actually possible!” shouted the adrenaline junkie with a substantial surge of adrenaline traveling up his spine.

“The first solution means that all these numbers are prime ('=1' means true),” he typed out an example for his own personal notes as he descended to the ground:

isprime(24108001)
= 1
isprime(241080001)
= 1
isprime(2410800001)
= 1
isprime(24108000001)
= 1
isprime(241080000001)

= 1
isprime(2410800000001)
= 1
isprime(24108000000001)
= 1

As he glided further and further down to earth, suspended in the thin air only by his parachute, more solutions continued appearing on his smart-phone:

43115464, 51114763, 55615987, 62565496, 67003048, 75987576, 86029125, ...

"Goddamn!" shouted the adrenaline junkie as he felt another blast of adrenaline assault his brain and spinal column, "these motherfreakers must be infinite!" He watched in amazement as even more solutions arrived:

92544459, 92858227, 97998817, 100406425, 105835849, 113825712, 132596107, ...

"How can this be possible?" he shouted. "How can there be so many solutions?" The adrenaline soared through his veins with each new solution that revealed itself:

146719566, 148523074, 154031325, 162623734, 168355278, 172741597, 175930279, ...

"Jesus, I am going to be forced to conjecture that this form of prime is infinite. There are so many it's amazing!"

The adrenaline junkie felt truly wonderful gliding down to the ground examining his computational number theory problem. Finally his feet hit the earth with a substantial thud but he stayed on his feet. He paused and looked at his smart-phone as it found even more solutions:

508287045, 510755182, 521195374, 539625534, 565492858, 567359226, 574480935, ...

The adrenaline junkie smiled broadly as he saved the numbers in a file so he could later explore them at home and eventually submit them to one of his favorite number theory web sites. The last solution looked so interesting he had to stop and compute out exactly what the number meant in terms of generating primes:

isprime(57448093501)
= 1
isprime(574480935001)
= 1
isprime(5744809350001)
= 1
isprime(57448093500001)
= 1
isprime(574480935000001)
= 1
isprime(5744809350000001)
= 1
isprime(57448093500000001)
= 1

isprime(5744809350000000001)
= 1

“Wow, that's one more than I originally programmed! There were only supposed to be seven!” He stared at the glorious stack of numbers and noticed there was indeed an extra solution that he had not originally programmed. The adrenaline junkie took intense pleasure in staring at the gleaming stack of primes before him. Finally he put his smart-phone in his pocket and gathered up his parachute and ran over to his friend who was waiting in a van many yards away.

The next few parachute jumps did not go so well for the adrenaline junkie. With each successive one, the spurt of adrenaline he felt seemed to lessen more and more. Until finally during a big jump from a stealth bomber near the stratosphere, he felt barely a tingle of adrenaline rushing through his body as he jumped.

But when he broke out his smart-phone and began attacking a number theory problem on the way down, he felt several strong rushes as he explored various numbers and their properties.

He realized his computational number theory thrills did not rely on possibly faulty parachutes or climbing high buildings illegally or paying large amounts to pilots to risk his life. It was a much healthier hobby all around.

So the adrenaline junkie decided he'd had enough. He

was going to call it a day. Jumping from airplanes and off skyscrapers was now officially over and he was only going to devote the rest of his time on earth to doing computational number theory problems.

He wanted to live a safe life on the ground from now on and spend it happily with his smart-phone running programs and exploring the wonderful world of numbers and submitting his interesting results to web sites for the rest of his days.

CASINOS AND POW-WOWS

she asked me if i
wanted to go
to the casino
and then
a pow-wow afterward

i told her
i didn't think
i would feel too comfortable
going to those things

she said: “Wow, you really
miss out on a lot
in life,
don't you?”

her comment
hit me
hard,
and made me
think

at 18, after being
inspired by
Jim Morrison,
i discovered
literature and books
and an
ENTIRELY NEW
WORLD
OPENED UP FOR ME

later, in my mid-20s
after being inspired by
biographies of
famous mathematicians
and pop math books,
even certain movies,
i discovered
number theory
and other "types"
of mathematics,
once again an
ENTIRELY NEW
GLORIOUS WORLD
OPENED UP FOR ME
TO EXPLORE AND
INDULGE IN

later still, in my mid-30s
after playing electric guitar
for many years
and being continually
frustrated
by flake-outs
and bands always
breaking up
for petty reasons,
i discovered
home-recording
via computer software
which made it
quick and easy
to record your
own music tracks,
then share them
via the internet.
once again,
an **AMAZING NEW**
WONDERFUL
WORLD OPENED
ITS DOORS
WIDE-OPEN
FOR ME

how could i explain
these ***WORLDS***
to this woman
who said i
was missing out on
life because I did not
want to go to
casinos and pow-wows?

i didn't try

the worlds I mentioned
are harder to get into
because you have to
BRING SOMETHING
SUBSTANTIAL
OF YOURSELF TO THEM,
you can't just passively
absorb them.
you have to **GO OUT**
and **MEET THEM** at least
half-way
with your
brain,
and imagination,
and perhaps
a little bit of
talent,
if you have any.

so i didn't attempt
to explain to her
these amazing **WORLDS**
that i had access to,
and that she was
barred from
permanently, for
her entire life.

i knew it would
be useless

but in the end,
i think
she
is the one
missing out.

MYSTICAL SYMBOLICS

X?X?X?X?X?X?X?X?X?X?X?X?X?X?X?X?X?X?X?X?X?
!~
+-
(*) (*) (*) (*) (*) (*) (*) (*) (*) (*) (*) (*) (*) (*)
987654321987654321987654321987654321987654
111111111111111111111111111111111111111111
$#
`^`^`^`^`^`^`^`^`^`^`^`^`^`^`^`^`^`^`^`^`^

X?X?X?X?X?X?X?X?X?X?X?X?X?X?X?X?X?X?X?X?X?
!~
235711235711235711235711235711235711235711
+-
(*) (*) (*) (*) (*) (*) (*) (*) (*) (*) (*) (*) (*) (*)
111111111111111111111111111111111111111111
$#
`^`^`^`^`^`^`^`^`^`^`^`^`^`^`^`^`^`^`^`^`^

987654321987654321987654321987654321987654
!~
+-
(*) (*) (*) (*) (*) (*) (*) (*) (*) (*) (*) (*) (*) (*)
111111111111111111111111111111111111111111
X?X?X?X?X?X?X?X?X?X?X?X?X?X?X?X?X?X?X?X?X?
235711235711235711235711235711235711235711
$#
`^`^`^`^`^`^`^`^`^`^`^`^`^`^`^`^`^`^`^`^`^

!~
(*) (*) (*) (*) (*) (*) (*) (*) (*) (*) (*) (*) (*) (*)
X?X?X?X?X?X?X?X?X?X?X?X?X?X?X?X?X?X?X?X?X?

FINDING A REAL ZEN MASTER

Raymond had been studying Zen Buddhism for a couple of years, and he'd finally arrived at a point when he badly wanted to find a genuine Zen master. But because he lived in a small redneck town full of hypocritical Christians, it seemed nearly impossible.

Raymond was studying Zen because he wanted total control over his mind – and to help him solve intense math problems. He didn't want to suffer from his own delusions anymore; he wanted to understand his true self; he wanted his mind to be clear and he wanted to see reality as it truly was/is – but he also hoped to solve one of the Millennium math problems and collect a million bucks.

Every morning Raymond would walk two miles to an old bridge to meditate and think about mathematics. He had read about walking meditation so he would practice that along the way to the bridge. Once there, he would sit down and cross his legs, hold his hands together with his thumbs lightly touching, and try to think about a way to prove the Riemann Hypothesis.

He would practice watching his breath, and counting the breaths, while attempting to stop the constant trivial thoughts streaming into his mind, and allow the important ones (hopefully about number theory) to pour forth.

When a mundane thought would arise, he would watch it without judgment, label it, then let it go. He had practiced this technique enough now that he could completely release most thoughts from his mind. He would focus on counting his breaths, rarely losing track of the count, and not getting distracted by random thoughts.

Meditation was hard work. It required a lot of concentration. But he felt it was worth it. After meditating in the morning, Raymond noticed he felt more peaceful and could concentrate on math better throughout the day. He also noticed he had moments of deep tranquility come over him at unusual times for no discernible reason.

Raymond also liked to practice opening up his third eye, which he thought would be the key to him attaining true math genius. He would change the position of his hands, form a circle with thumb and forefinger, then on the exhale he would make a medium-pitched note that vibrated the center of his forehead where his third eye was located. He would make the humming noise for a long time, while also doing many exhalations and really focusing on opening up his third eye. He wanted to release the mathematical power that lurked there, but only to work on number theory that had little real-world applications, not to create weapons of any sort. He wanted the intuition and divine wisdom that dwelled inside his third eye to manifest itself in his daily life and help him solve an important math problem with a substantial monetary reward.

One day while meditating atop the bridge, Raymond noticed a strange man underneath the bridge squatting by a rock. The man looked homeless, with disheveled red hair, and he wore a ratty set of brown coveralls. Raymond rose from his sitting position on the bridge and walked down the side and called out, “Hello sir, do you need any help?”

“What type of meditation are you practicing up there?” said the homeless looking man.

“Oh, are you familiar with meditation?” Raymond asked, continually walking closer.

“A little bit.”

Raymond stopped and stood in front of the homeless man who had brown crooked teeth. He didn't seem dangerous: he held a good-natured look in his eye. Up close his red hair looked really wild, long and sticking out in all directions. The man seemed somewhat guarded and Raymond could tell he didn't want to shake hands. So Raymond looked away and started to explain his meditation practice: “Well, basically I do three different types. One, the basis of my practice, is just counting the breaths and when a thought comes in I try to let it go and refocus on counting breaths. The second type is where I try to open up my third eye. I hold a different posture with my hands and make a humming note and try to vibrate the center of my forehead where my third eye is located. The third type is just something I came up with on my own: I like to walk out into the woods, go to a place where it's not easy to sit down, and I stand in a power pose. With my hands on hips, legs slightly wide, eyes closed, head tilted upward toward the heavens, I exhale normally, but on the inhale I imagine ALL THE POWER OF THE ENTIRE UNIVERSE entering my body through the top of my head. There is a sort of lightness combined with a moderate feeling of ecstasy, when I can do it correctly, as I try to pull all the power of the world down into myself. On certain good days I can REALLY PULL that feeling into me, but on bad days it's a struggle to feel the ecstasy and it just doesn't happen. I'm doing all this because I want to turn myself into a math genius."

After listening to the long-winded explanation, the homeless man stared down at the ground with a deeply puzzled look on his face. He scratched at his mop of wild red hair.

"Is anything wrong?" said Raymond.

"Oh, no. Those are good techniques. But I have a question for you: **Where do we go when we die?**"

Raymond sighed heavily. "Yes, death. One of the deepest questions. I've been meaning to meditate upon that for awhile now, but haven't gotten around to it yet. So right now I have no clue, where do you think we go?"

The homeless man looked deadly serious and said: "After years of pondering it, I finally got an answer the other day. To me it seems we are just bundles of energy, and when we die all the energy inside us travels out and takes up residence in another bodily form somewhere else, say on another planet in another solar system."

"Okay, I'm following you so far. Go on..."

"There are many other planets surrounding stars in the universe that are the exact distance as the Earth is from our sun, correct? Meaning they are probably capable of supporting life just as ours does."

"Sounds reasonable. The universe is infinite. There must be a lot of other planets in the universe that can sustain life forms such as ours."

"So instead of going to heaven or hell, who is to say that when we die we don't just get reborn on another planet and have no memory of the earthly life we lived previously? And of course our new life will be nothing like the one we are living now in any way. Also our bodily forms will be much different than the ones we have presently."

Raymond scratched his face. "Sounds plausible. But I don't see what this has to do with Zen or meditation?"

"It doesn't really. It's just a question I've struggled with over the years. Actually this thought arose while I was engaged in a meditation session one day, and I could not block it, or let it go, from my mind."

"I see. So you also practice meditation?"

The homeless man squinted. "I've meditated for many years. Which is why I stopped under this bridge. I could see you were meditating and it brought back memories of my own practice. Would you like to learn one of my techniques that I developed, which is almost guaranteed to help you reach enlightenment within one year of it being performed?"

"Yes, but keep in mind, I mainly want mathematical ability. Will your technique help me with that?"

"Math is worthless."

Raymond's face turned red. But he didn't want to argue with the homeless man. He changed the subject: "Are you enlightened?"

"I used to be. It comes and goes. It's really difficult to hang on to. Here, watch this. Take just a few steps closer to me."

When Raymond got close, the homeless man raised both his dirty hands above his head and Raymond looked up at them. Next the man raised his right leg quickly and kicked Raymond in the groin but not too hard, and once Raymond was doubled over from the pain, the unknown man slapped the sides of his face three times: **right hand! left hand! right hand!** extremely fast and hard.

At that moment Raymond raised back up and looked into the sky, and he felt enlightenment and true realization descend upon him in full force: feelings of pure bliss and ecstasy and emotional freedom washed over his entire body, intense sensations he'd never felt before.

Initially he thought the strange man was attacking him to

steal his money, but when he felt the enlightenment come, he realized the man was a practitioner of the Rinzai school and was using a violent "shock technique" to make him attain full enlightenment. It seemed to work. For a minute or so, Raymond couldn't speak. Finally he managed to say: "Oh my God. I mean, Buddha. I just had an enlightenment experience."

"Don't get too excited. It won't last long. That's not true enlightenment. It's just a taste of what is to come, if you're lucky. That only works on people who have been meditating for long periods of time and are on the verge of true enlightenment. If you keep meditating a few more years, you will surely get the real enlightenment. And even then, you will have to work very hard to hold on to it because it may not last. In no time you will probably find yourself returning to your normal human foibles. Such as your cravings for 'math fame' and other trivialities."

"Is math really worthless?" Raymond asked.

"Yes. Forget about it. There are many more important things to focus on."

Raymond didn't know what else to say. He hated having his dream of solving one of the Millennium math problems shattered. He needed to get a million dollars somehow, he was tired of being broke all the time. Raymond wondered how this bizarre homeless man had this much knowledge about the world and enlightenment. But he didn't want to bother him with any more questions. Raymond turned and looked down into the creek below. The water was calm and peaceful. He felt he was connected to the water – and to the nature around him – in a way that he had never before experienced.

Finally Raymond's curiosity got the better of him. “Can I ask how you know all of this?”

“I studied Zen for a few years in Tibet.”

“Can you give me some kind of proof?”

The man began chanting in a foreign language. It sounded so strange Raymond knew it had to be genuine. Some of it sounded like chants he had heard in a Buddhist documentary that he'd watched on Netflix, except the homeless man's voice sounded lower and more distorted, like an electric guitar.

“Amazing. Now I really believe you. Have you read the *Diamond Sutra*?”

“Of course.”

“I have been reading that one a lot lately. Trying to embed it in my mind.”

The homeless man suddenly grinned knowingly. “Try this technique. Tomorrow when you read it, use your mind while holding the state that you had before you knew how to read.”

“Ahhh...” Raymond's eyes lit up as he became absorbed in that thought. “Yes. Sounds interesting, I'll try that. Do you also know about koan practice?"

"Yes. Ask me a koan."

"How can you, as the Buddha, produce five million dollars in a black bucket?"

"What I want, money can't buy."

"Such as?"

"Such as this:

1. Good health and a fit physique
2. Musical ability and talent
3. Writing ability and talent

Those are the three things I want most in this world."

"But doesn't having enlightenment erase those desires?" Raymond said.

"No."

"How can you say that? It goes against Buddhist philosophy. Everything that it teaches. The elimination of desire is the salvation from suffering. And you say math is worthless, but yet you want writing ability and musical talent. Aren't those things just as worthless as mathematics?"

No answer. The homeless man simply nodded in the negative and looked away with a withdrawn look on his face, refusing to explain anything further.

“Ask me what Zen is,” the homeless man finally said.

“What is Zen?”

“A dried shit stick.”

“No it's not, it's Zamboodi,” said Raymond.

“What's that?”

“One time my mother misheard me saying 'Zen Buddhism' – she thought I was saying the word 'Zamboodi' – and she started telling all her friends that I was practicing a strange religion called Zamboodi in the garage all the time and they were becoming very worried about me because they were supposedly Christians. They thought I was practicing some form of black magic.”

“Hahaha, Zamboodi, I like that. Well, I guess I should be going now.” He turned and took a few steps.

Raymond was surprised at his sudden departure. “Will I see you again?”

“Perhaps. But you don't need me. I gave you all the tools you need to succeed with Zen.”

“Are you a real Zen master?”

“No.”

"Well, thanks for telling me about the life force canceling out and reappearing on another planet in another galaxy. That's an amazing concept."

"You are welcome."

And the homeless man with the wild red hair and dirty brown coveralls walked away, and Raymond never laid eyes on him again.

About the Author

Jason Earls is a computational number theorist, guitarist, and concrete poet who specializes in employing the Gongorism literary style to write poignant mathematical treatises, experimental novels, technical manuals, concrete prime-poems, and Southern Gothic works. He is the author of *Math Freak, That Man is a Sinner, How to Become a Guitar Player from Hell, The Lowbrow Experimental Mathematician, Red Zen, Concrete Calculator-Word Primes, the Underground Guitar Handbook, You Will Be Amazed by the Entertainment, Mathematical Bliss, Heartless Bastard In Ecstasy, the Primitive Knife Manual, A Cringe-Meister in the Bathos-Shere, Cocoon of Terror, I Sin Every Number, Zombies of the Red Descent, Death Knocks,* and *0.136101521283655...* all available at Amazon.com and other fine online book stores. His fiction and mathematical work have been published in Red Scream, M-Brane SF, three of Clifford Pickover's books, Mathworld.com, AlienSkin, Recreational and Educational Computing, Thirteen, Prime Curios, the Online Encyclopedia of Integer Sequences, OG's Speculative Fiction, Nocturnal Ooze, and other publications. He currently resides in Oklahoma with his wife, Christine. Contact him at zevi_35711@yahoo.com

Special thanks to Christine Earls, Dorlynn Earls, and Chad Ian Earls for their support during the writing of this book.

Music tracks by Jason Earls featuring his guitar playing can be heard here:
http://www.youtube.com/user/machguitar9

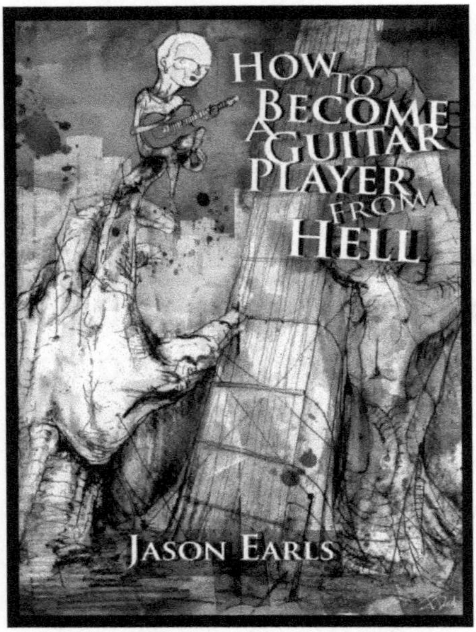

HOW TO BECOME A GUITAR PLAYER FROM HELL

Have you ever wanted to learn how to play the electric guitar? Have you ever been curious about scales, arpeggios, modes, chords (both simple & sophisticated), harmonics (natural & artificial). How about "outside playing" and never-before published techniques such as the "wah-wham method" or the avant-garde "lizard down the throat" technique? Whatever the case may be, the excellent instructional guitar book, How to Become a Guitar Player from Hell, covers nearly every playing method used by modern day guitar virtuosos and explains them in simple terms anyone can understand. Available at your favorite online book store.

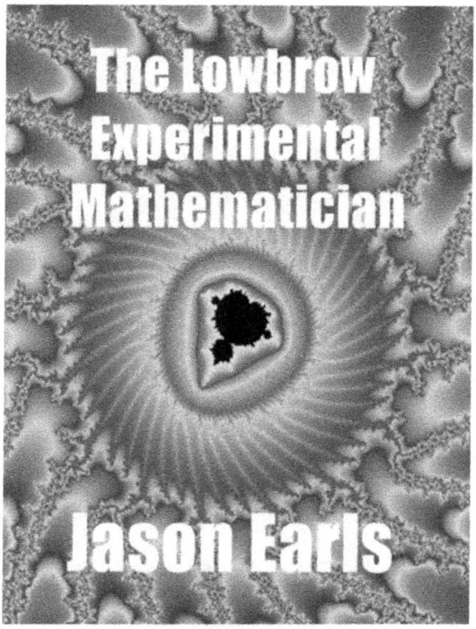

The Lowbrow Experimental Mathematician

A book of cutting-edge number theory articles plus mathematically inspired short fiction and experimental texts. Prime hunters, psychics, Horace S. Uhler, psychos living in condemned funeral parlors, midnight hackers, the Kiwa Hirsuta crustacean, Frenicle de Bessy, unusual poems, Genghis Khan, solutions to y^3 = x^2 + k, Andy Warhol, programming languages, concrete primes, zebra irrational numbers, and near misses to Fermat's Last Theorem. The *Lowbrow Experimental Mathematician* has plenty of compelling material to leave you inspired and entertained for many years.

UNDERGROUND GUITAR HANDBOOK

If you've ever wanted to learn the newest "underground" and innovative guitar methods, this handbook is for you. Filled with cutting-edge and avant-garde guitar techniques, the Underground Guitar Handbook contains detailed explanations and musical examples of such topics as, four-finger licks, unusual scales, diminished licks, tremolo bar flutters and gurgles, the wah-wham method, tritones and flatted fifths, Shawn Lane's "impossible" chord, speed-picking licks, pedal point phrases, new hardware ideas, atonal patterns, mysticism, finger-tapping licks, and much more. Links to the author's youtube videos in which he performs the techniques are also provided; (plus a handful of musical short stories for additional entertainment). For learning the most cutting-edge guitar techniques (many never before published), this manual is all you will ever need. Search for it on Amazon.

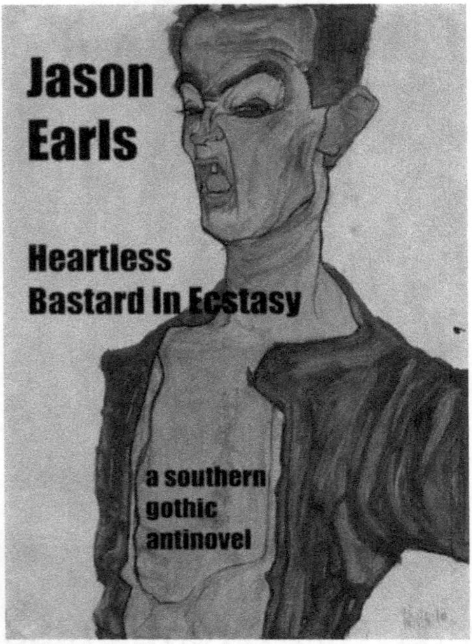

HEARTLESS BASTARD IN ECSTASY

Clyde and Theresa, living their shattered lives in a small town. Sad, desperate, lonely, heart broken. Working crappy jobs, having lascivious sexual encounters with perfect strangers, wandering through graveyards, drinking cough syrup in night clubs, playing with strange chemical compositions, praying in flophouses, and striving for the forbidden in every possible way. What else could they do? Not much. Lurking within this southern gothic antinovel is an entire universe of abnormality, with emotional contraptions situated between the text and reader for maximum sensory enhancement.

NUMBERS FOR WITTGENSTEIN

Chapters: Preface, Wittgenstein's Iteration Problem, Ten 10s Not Yet Found in Pi or Other Constants, On the Divisors of the Number 1 + 10^40 + 100^40, My Struggle With Mathematical Philosophy, Various Results with the Partition Function, Computations on Numbers of the Form e^Pi*sqrt(n), Aliquot Chain Computations, Two Excerpts from "Cocoon of Terror", On Nontrivial Palindromic Divisors of "Pi", Meditation and Visualizing Proth's Theorem, Fifteen Easy Ways to Boost Your Intelligence, Excerpt from the Novel "Red Zen", Computations and Remarks on a Pascal-Like Function, Letter to Ludwig, About the Author.

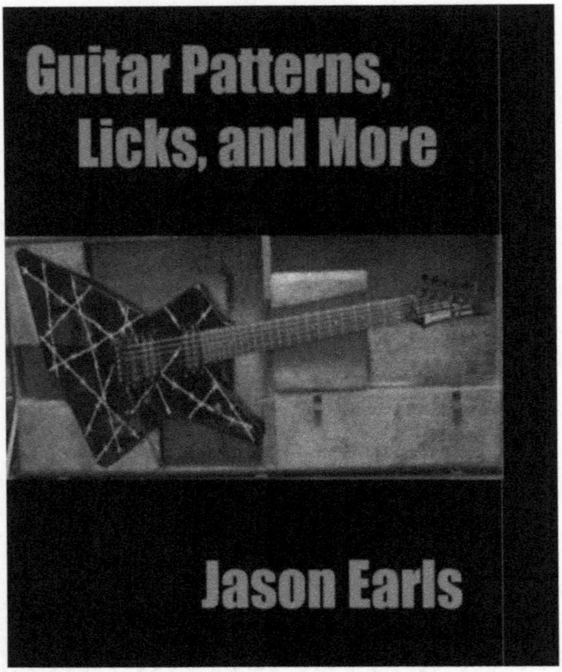

GUITAR PATTERNS, LICKS, AND MORE

Topics include: Holdsworth style licks, outside patterns, diminished licks, Niccolo Paganini, Sonny Sharrock, chromatic licks, wide stretches, string skipping, Johann Sebastian Bach, finger tapping, sweep arpeggios, John McLaughlin, wide intervals, finger exercises, bending strings, mysticism and the guitar, fiction related to band experiences, and more. http://tinyurl.com/k55wlqp

RED ZEN

(Taught for three years at Virginia Tech University by Professor Robert Siegle). Saul Summerblend has a bizarre memory problem; and his Zen master, Bodhee, says he should travel to the dwarf planet Ceres to fix it. Along the way Saul meets a thirty-foot magic square whose diagonals and rows sum to 666, encounters a group of drunken Vikings and evil dwarves, works some campy mathematics and overhears amusing CB radio conversations, fights a visionary with a penchant for wrestling masks and flipping off cars all day on main street, invents neologisms like deemkrite and freeganidge. He also learns of a mystical book called 'Red Zen: Way of the Butterfly' and attempts to solve a few koans about kangaroos, split toe nails, and carts filled with hatchets. Will Saul fix his strange memory problem? Will he even make it back to Earth alive?

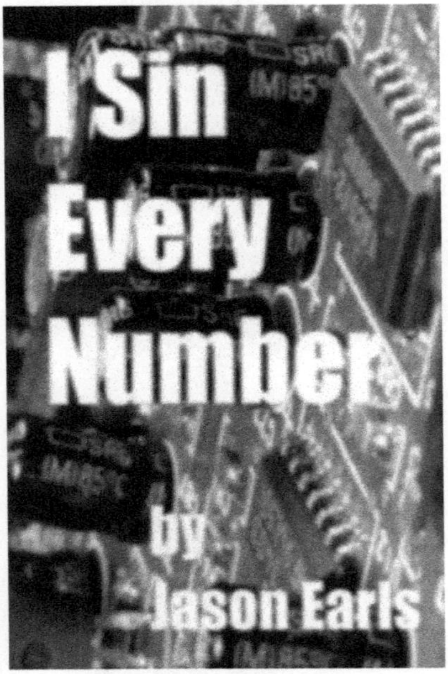

I SIN EVERY NUMBER

Formerly 3/4's of the infamous novel, If{Sid_Vicious == TRUE && Alan_Turing == TRUE, ERROR_Cyberpunk();} praised by Cory Doctorow as an "awesome title," this version has been extensively revised with new material added, plus there's an extensive introduction explaining the novel's origins. **Description**: Computer problems. We've all had them and they are always a pain. Sabrina, a freelance programmer, has recently been experiencing computer problems worse than anything she's ever encountered before. Disturbing messages and unknown symbols and eerie text. She doesn't know if they're merely a practical joke or actual signals from another solar system. But she's determined to find out. And Dr. Mwang is no help. He's Sabrina's best friend as well as a supergenius, but she doesn't understand why he refuses to investigate her problem and why his attitude toward her has suddenly changed...

by Jason Earls

A CRINGE-MEISTER IN THE BATHOS-SPHERE

Max Reynolds failed as a writer.

Yet Max Reynolds continues to write.

He must write every day or he will sink into an almost catatonic depression.

This is Max Reynolds' story, told mainly through samples of his writing.

COMPUTING WITH FERMAT

Chapters: On Fermat's Factorization Method, Fermat Concrete Prime, $x^n + y^n$ = Triangular, Brilliant Base-2 Pseudoprimes, Reciprocal Primes from Factors of Repunits, On the Diophantine Equation $x^2 + y^3 = z^4$, Fun with the Sqrt(n) Primality Test, Three Cubes that Sum to a Fibonacci Number, Bernard Frenicle de Bessy and A New "Problem" in his Style, On the Divisors of $2^{(2^n)} + 2$ and $2^{(2^n)} + 4$, Near-Misses of Fermat's Last Theorem.

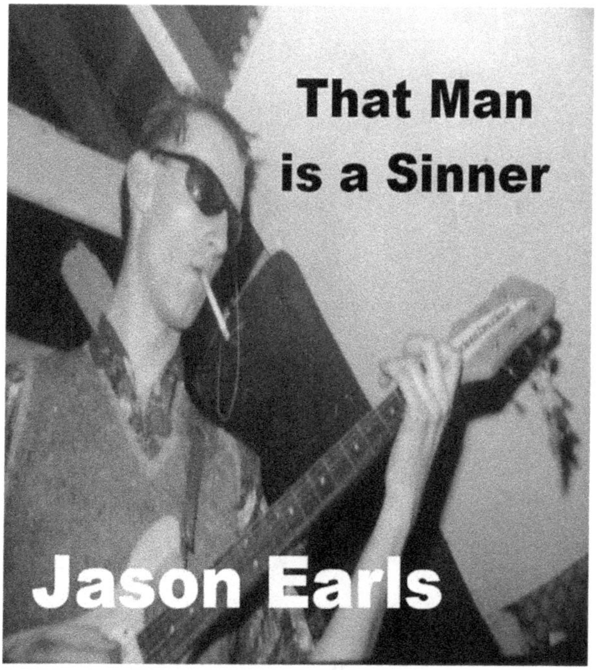

That Man Is a Sinner

Ingenious tickling machines, one hundred point bucks, knife fights at class reunions, death metal bands having deep philosophy discussions, law-breaking poster tricks, a blues guitarist meeting Eric Clapton in the form of Barack Obama, flying quad-runners, world record back busters, *That Man is a Sinner* by Jason Earls has it all.

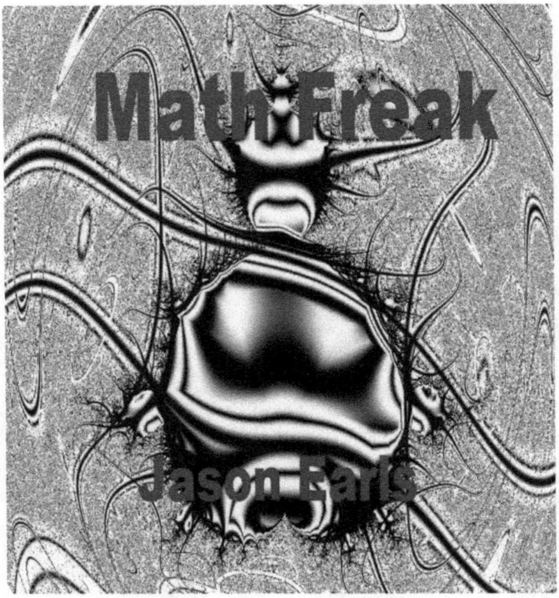

MATH FREAK

Contents: Preface, Bar-Hopping and Palindromic Divisors (fiction), Variations of Brocard's Conjecture, Pell's Equation and Jesus's Number, Note On Reversible Prime Numbers (Base-10), 379009*n and Digital Sums, Mersenne's Mistake (fiction), On Brocard's Factorial Square Problem, Computations on the Reverse-and-Add 196-Problem, Brilliant Harshad Numbers are Finite, Computations on a Certain Sequence of Primes (with a Rant), Stumbling Onto an Elliptic Curve, On the Sigma(Phi(n)) Function and Some Related Sequences, Excerpts from "I Sin Every Number" (fiction), Weird Brilliant Number Sequences, Prime = 10^14508 - 10^14490-1 , Building a Machine to Find Arithmetic Progressions of Primes (fiction), About the Author.

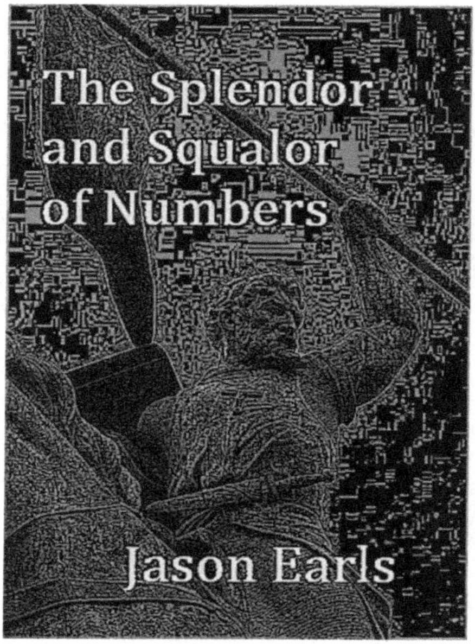

The Splendor and Squalor of Numbers

Preface, The Power of Compound Interest, Fifth Power Near-Misses of Fermat's Last Theorem, The Technological Singularity, Supercomputers and the Next Prime After n!+n, Nothing Unreal Exists, 900..700..500..300..1 Primes and Andy Warhol, Data and a Conjecture Concerning Twin Primes, Revrepfigits Sequence from OEIS, On Zebra Irrational Numbers z(5*10^n) and Others, Art Brut Prime, Fibonacci Brilliants and Partial Fibonacci Brilliants, On 10n+1 Numbers and Undulating Primes, R9(n)^R9(n) Ending Digits, Star Prime, My Workout Partner, A Mind That Is Still, About the Author.

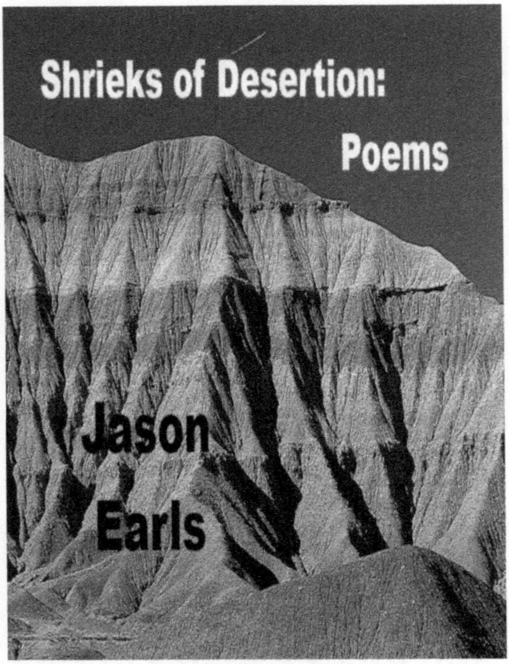

Poems: The Blank Page, Motel Man, Kissing the Wrong Person Good Night, Champion Long Jumper, Adding Numbers, Studying Poetry, Fermat, Destroy Your Enemies by Making Them Your Friends, Let's Get the Party Started, The Desire for Logic, Young and Wasted, History of a Bearded Homeless Man, Squeeze the Bleeding Earth, How to Get a Million Dollars, Spectacular, Paganini, Tablature, A Long Weird Word, Felonies, Mysticism, Realist, Rotate the Digits, Childish Junkie Scrawl, Too Many Charlatans, Hot Molten Sulfur, After You Fail, You're Much More Attractive, It Is Very Disappointing, Arnold Schwarzenneger, Weightlifting, Freak Scale, Interweb Gonzoid Superhero, Trash Man Stereo Adjustor, Crushing Cars, Cowboy Yodel Auction, Campiness, At The Skating Rink, Evel Knievel, and more...

http://tinyurl.com/l9amtqh

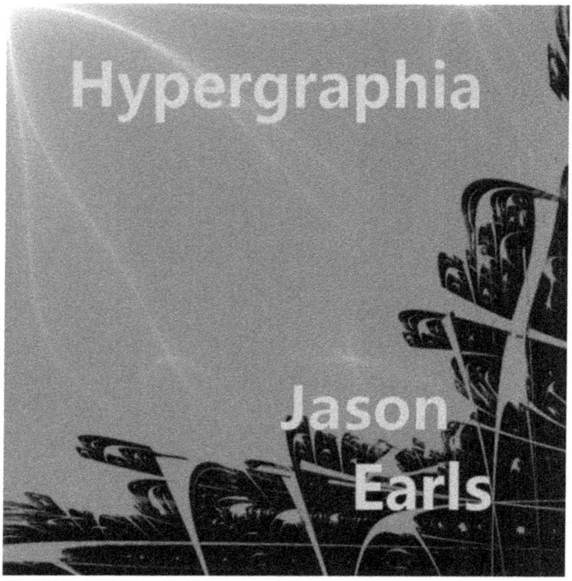

Preface, The Minimalist Concrete Poet, The Zen Master's New Method, Hypergraphia, Contribute A Verse, On Becoming Blinded by Our Obsessions, Articulation, What is Zen?, On the Importance of Having Goals, One-Word and Minimal Poems, Could We Build the Egyptian Pyramids Today?, Death of the Long Blue C**k, A Dried Shit Stick, Rant on Fitness, The Young Punk and the Old Bartender, A Scientific Discovery I Will Make Someday, Alpha Male Poem, Nervous Breakdown, A Man-Child's Dream Come True, Constant Baby Talk, Meditation and Evil Levitation, Death Metal Kid, Face Down in the Library Parking Lot, Concrete Primes, An Important Literary Discovery, and more... Jason Earls is a guitarist, computational number theorist, and concrete poet. He is the author of the Underground Guitar Handbook, Numbers for Wittgenstein, Red Zen, Math Freak, How to Become a Guitar Player from Hell, and other books.

www.ingramcontent.com/pod-product-compliance
Lightning Source LLC
Chambersburg PA
CBHW051245050326
40689CB00007B/1067
* 9 7 8 1 3 1 2 8 3 4 8 7 3 *